WITNESSES TO THE JOHN F. KENNEDY ASSASSINATION

Books LLC®, Wiki Series, Memphis, USA, 2011. ISBN: 9781155839844. www.booksllc.net
Copyright: http://creativecommons.org/licenses/by-sa/3.0/deed.en

Table of Contents

Abraham Zapruder	2
Babushka Lady	3
Badge man	4
Charles Brehm	5
Clint Hill	6
David Powers	7
Emmett Hudson	7
Faye Chism	7
George Jefferies	8
Gordon Arnold	8
Howard Brennan	9
Hurchel Jacks	9
Ike Altgens	10
Jack Valenti	12
Jacqueline Kennedy Onassis	14
James M. Chaney	22
James Tague	22
Jean Hill	23
Jerry Haynes	24
John Connally	25
Kenneth O'Donnell	29
Lee Bowers	30
Lee Harvey Oswald	31
Linda Willis	40
Marie Muchmore	40
Marilyn Sitzman	41
Mary Moorman	42
Nellie Connally	42
Orville Nix	43
Phillip Willis	44
Ralph Yarborough	44
Robert MacNeil	46
Rosemary Willis	47
Roy Kellerman	48
Umbrella Man (JFK assassination)	49
William Allen Harper	49
William Greer	50

Introduction

Purchase of this book entitles you to a free trial membership in the publisher's book club at www.booksllc.net. (Time limited offer.) Simply enter the barcode number from the back cover onto the membership form. The book club entitles you to select from hundreds of thousands of books at no additional charge. You can also download a digital copy of this and related books to read on the go. Simply enter the title or subject onto the search form to find them.

Each chapter in this book ends with a URL to a hyperlinked online version. Type the URL exactly as it appears. If you change the URL's capitalization it won't work. Use the online version to access related pages, websites, footnotes, tables, color photos, updates. Click the version history tab to see the chapter's contributors. Click the edit link to suggest changes.

A large and diverse editor base collaboratively wrote the book, not a single author. After a long process of discussion and debate, the chapters gradually took on a neutral point of view reached through consensus. Additional editors expanded and contributed to chapters striving to achieve balance and comprehensive coverage. This reduced the regional or cultural bias found in many other books and provided access and breadth on subject matter otherwise little documented.

Abraham Zapruder

Abraham Zapruder (right) describes to WFAA-TV's Jay Watson the President's head wound on live television hours after the assassination.

Abraham Zapruder (May 15, 1905 – August 30, 1970) was an American manufacturer of women's clothing. He was filming with a home-movie camera as U.S. President John F. Kennedy's motorcade passed through Dealey Plaza, Dallas, Texas on November 22, 1963, and unexpectedly captured the President's assassination on what came to be known as the *Zapruder Film*.

Personal background

Zapruder was born into a Russian-Jewish family in the city of Kovel in Ukraine (at that time under the Russian Empire). He received only four years of formal education in Russia. In 1920 amid the turmoil of the Russian Civil War, his family immigrated to the United States, settling in Brooklyn, New York. Studying English at night, he found work as a clothing pattern maker in Manhattan's garment district. He and his wife Lillian married in 1933 and had two children.

In 1941 Zapruder moved to Dallas to work for Nardis, a local sportswear company. In 1954 he co-founded Jennifer Juniors, Inc., producing the Chalet and Jennifer Juniors brands. His offices were in the Dal-Tex Building, directly across the street east of the Texas School Book Depository.

Zapruder died of stomach cancer in 1970 in Dallas. A 2007 film, *Frame 313*, tells the story of his life.

Witness to Kennedy assassination

Inadvertent filming of assassination

Abraham Zapruder's camera, in the collection of the US National Archives

Zapruder considered himself a Democrat and was an admirer of President Kennedy. Not originally intending to bring his camera to the motorcade, at the insistence of his assistant he retrieved it from home before going to Dealey Plaza.

The camera was an 8 mm Bell & Howell Zoomatic Director Series Model 414 PD—top of the line when it was purchased in 1962. Zapruder waited atop a concrete pedestal along Elm Street, his receptionist Marilyn Sitzman prepared to steady him from behind, and began filming as the President's limousine turned onto Elm Street in front of the Book Depository. The next 26.6 seconds were captured on 486 frames of Kodak Kodachrome II safety film.

Walking back to his office amid the confusion following the shots, Zapruder encountered *Dallas Morning News* reporter Harry McCormack, who was acquainted with Agent Forrest Sorrels of the Secret Service's Dallas office. McCormack offered to bring Sorrels to Zapruder's office. Zapruder continued to his office where he sent his assistant Lillian Rogers to find a Secret Service agent, in case McCormack failed to find Sorrels. McCormack did find Sorrels, outside the Sheriff's office at Main and Houston, and together they went to Zapruder's office.

Zapruder agreed to give the film to Sorrels on the condition it would be used only for investigation of the assassination. The group took the film to the television station WFAA to be developed.

After it was realized that WFAA was unable to develop Zapruder's footage, in the late afternoon it was taken to Eastman Kodak's Dallas processing plant where it was immediately developed. Because under the Kodachrome process, different equipment is required for duplication than for simple development, around 6:30 p.m. the developed original was taken to the Jamieson Film Company, where three additional copies were exposed; these were returned to Kodak around 8 p.m. for processing. Zapruder kept the original, plus one copy, and gave the other two copies to Sorrels, who sent them to Secret Service headquarters in Washington.

Television interview

While at WFAA, Zapruder described on live television what he had seen:

Sale of rights

Late that evening, Zapruder was contacted at home by Richard Stolley, an editor at *Life* magazine (and first editor of the future *People* magazine). They arranged to meet the following morning to view the film, after which Zapruder sold the print rights to *Life* magazine for $50,000. The following day (November 24), *Life* purchased all rights to the film for a total of $150,000 (equivalent to $1 million in 2007). (Zapruder gave the first $25,000 to the widow of Dallas policeman J.D. Tippit, who had been killed confronting Lee Harvey Oswald in the hours after the assassination.)

The night after the assassination, Zapruder is said to have had a nightmare in which he saw a booth in Times Square advertising "See the President's head explode!" He determined that, while he was willing to make money from the film, he did not want the public to see the full horror of what he had seen. Therefore, a condition of the sale to *Life* was that frame 313, showing the fatal shot, would be withheld.

Testimony

On November 22 United States PRS Special Agent Maxwell D. Phillips sent a hand-written memo to Secret Service head James Rowley, stating that, "According to Mr Zapruder the position of the assassin was behind Mr Zapruder." But in his testimony to the Warren Commission Zapruder was less certain: Zapruder added that he had assumed the shots came from behind him because the explosive wound on the side of the President's head was facing that direction, and because police officers ran to the area behind Zapruder.

He broke down and wept as he recalled the assassination, and did so again at the 1969 trial of Clay Shaw.
Source (edited): "http://en.wikipedia.org/wiki/Abraham_Zapruder"

Babushka Lady

In the 1963 assassination of President John F. Kennedy, **Babushka Lady** is a nickname for an unknown woman who might have photographed the events that occurred in Dallas' Dealey Plaza at the time President John F. Kennedy was shot. Her nickname arose from the headscarf she wore similar to scarves worn by elderly Russian women (бабушка – *babushka* – means "grandmother" or "old woman" in Russian).

Babushka Lady was seen to be holding a camera by eyewitnesses and was also seen in film accounts of the assassination (such as this Muchmore frame and Zapruder Frame 285). She was observed standing on the grass between Elm and Main streets and she can be seen in the Zapruder film as well as in the films of Orville Nix, Marie Muchmore, and Mark Bell (44 seconds and 49 seconds into the Bell film: even though the shooting had already taken place and most of her surrounding witnesses took cover, she can be seen still standing with the camera at her face). After the shootings, she crossed Elm Street and joined the crowd that went up the grassy knoll in search of a gunman. She is last seen in photographs walking east on Elm Street and neither she nor the film she may have taken have been positively identified.

Identity

The Babushka Lady never came forward. The police and the FBI did not find her, and the film shot from her position never turned up, despite a request by the FBI to local photo processors that they would be interested in any pictures or films of the assassination. Jack Harrison, a Kodak technician in Dallas, claimed to have developed on November 22, 1963, the day of the assassination, an out-of-focus color slide for a brunette in her late 30s that showed a view similar to the Babushka Lady's position.

Beverly Oliver

In 1970, a woman named Beverly Oliver came forward and claimed to be the Babushka Lady. She had worked in 1963 as a singer and dancer at a strip club that competed with Jack Ruby's Carousel Club. In 1994, she released a memoir chronicling the events of the day of Kennedy's assassination, but she has not been able to provide convincing proof she was there. Oliver says her film was taken by Federal agent Regis Kennedy and never returned.

Critics have noted a number of inconsistencies with her story, such as her alleged use of a model of camera that did not exist in 1963, and her claim to have positioned herself just behind Charles Brehm and his son, despite Brehm's statement that he and his son had hurried to that position at the last moment. Also, the fact that the Babushka lady appears to be a stout, middle-aged woman, whereas Oliver was 17 at the time of the assassination, tends to cast doubts on Oliver's claims.

Oliver was played by Lolita Davidovich in the 1991 film *JFK*, but is not portrayed as claiming to be the Babushka Lady. In the director's cut she is depicted as wearing a head scarf at Dealey Plaza and speaking of having given the film she shot to two men claiming to be FBI agents.

In the 1992 film *Ruby*, the character of Candy Cane, portrayed by Sherilyn Fenn, is shown in Dealey Plaza filming the motorcade and wearing a babushka scarf. Though the character is a singer and nightclub performer, there is no evidence that she is based in any meaningful way on Beverly Oliver.
Source (edited): "http://en.wikipedia.org/wiki/Babushka_Lady"

Badge man

Polaroid photo by Mary Moorman taken just after the fatal shot, showing the "Badge Man" (detail)

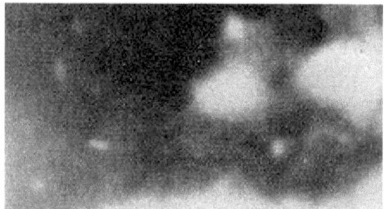

An enlargement of the "Badge Man" image

Badge Man is the name given to a photographic image that some President John F. Kennedy assassination researchers claim is a grassy knoll assassin seen within a Polaroid photograph that close witness Mary Moorman captured on November 22, 1963 within Dealey Plaza in Dallas, Texas. The photo sparked the conspiracy theory that three Dallas police officers killed Kennedy instead of Oswald.

The Photo

In the Moorman Polaroid photo (her fifth that day) is seen all of the Presidential limousine occupants, several other close witnesses (including Abraham Zapruder filming), two Dallas police motorcycle Presidential escorts, and much of the area comprising the grassy knoll. The photo has been calculated to have been captured between the Zapruder film equivalent concurrent frames of Z-315 and 316 (less than one-sixth of a second after President Kennedy's head first exploded at Z-313). On the actual Polaroid photo, the area that the Badge Man appears within is about one-quarter inch square.

In 1982 Gary Mack, the longtime curator and archivist for The Sixth Floor Museum at Dealey Plaza (the former Texas School Book Depository) first claimed to discover the "Badge Man" image. He labeled this image Badge Man because the image shows what may appear to be a uniformed police officer wearing dark clothing and his police patrolman's metal badge on his chest and his left shoulder crest curved police patrolman patch, his hatless short hair, and the majority of his Caucasian face. A whitish spot slightly obscuring the Badge Man face is claimed to be the visual remnant of an already fired weapon muzzle blast, the bullet from which if fired at President Kennedy from his right front would have had to pass over the 3.3 feet (1.0 m) high cement retaining wall.

Other researchers have claimed that the "Badge Man" image is the sun-reflected outline of a soda pop bottle sitting atop the cement retaining wall. Marilyn Sitzman, who was standing a few yards from the retaining wall, saw a young black couple eating lunch on a bench behind that wall, and heard a soda bottle crash just after the motorcade passed by. Photos and films immediately afterwards do show a bottle sitting atop the retaining wall.

The House Select Committee on Assassinations sent a high-quality negative of the photo to the Rochester Institute of Technology; after enlarging the photo, no evidence of a person on the retaining wall was found. The area around the stockade fence was so underexposed, that it was deemed impossible to examine.

In the mid-1980s, assassination researcher Jack White (who testified to the House Select Committee on Assassinations) enhanced the immediate photograph area of the "Badge Man" in contrast and brightness, then he enhanced further with what White has described as "clear photographic colored oils" to illustrate the "Badge Man". White's enhancement first appeared publicly in the 1988 documentary *The Men Who Killed Kennedy*.

To the anatomical right (photo left) of the supposed "Badge Man" some researchers claim there is also seen a second person, self-proclaimed witness Gordon Arnold, who claimed in 1978 that he was filming the motorcade while wearing his US Army uniform when a shot passed close to his left ear. A third person claimed by researchers to be seen is a construction hard hatted accomplice to "Badge Man's" anatomical left (photo right) facing the general direction of the book depository.

Also claimed seen in the Moorman Polaroid photo by many researchers is the hatted head of a person located about 13 feet (3.9 m) west of the grassy knoll stockade fence corner (a different location from the "Badge Man"). This image area is exactly the same area where several overpass witnesses stated they observed gunsmoke, where several of those gunsmoke witnesses (and other witnesses) immediately ran to, seeing no one but finding hundreds of footprints in the mud directly behind a station wagon backed up to the stockade fence that also had shoe-bottom mud scraped off onto the station wagon's rear bumper, cigarette butts, and muddy footprints 2.5 feet (0.75 m) up on a picket fence cross-beam support. This is also exactly the same location from which the second major Kennedy assassination government investigation, the House Select Committee on Assassinations, determined through scientific testing that one shot was fired.

Source (edited): "http://en.wikipedia.org/wiki/Badge_man"

Charles Brehm

Charles F. Brehm (1925-August 8, 1996) was a witness to the assassination of President John F. Kennedy within Dealey Plaza in Dallas Texas on November 22, 1963.

Charles F. Brehm and his 5-year-old son, Joe, were standing in the Dealey Plaza north infield grass, a few feet south of the south curb of Elm Street, across the street from Abraham Zapruder and the Dealey Plaza grassy knoll. They can both be clearly seen in the Zapruder film.

Brehm was a World War II veteran who served in the United States Army Rangers and fought on D-Day. He later also served in the Korean War.

When the Presidential limousine turned from Main Street onto Houston Street Brehm and his son watched from that intersections northwest side. After watching the turn, Brehm and his son quickly ran northwestward across the "north infield grass" towards the south curb of Elm Street to catch another glimpse of the President. They were standing close to the south curb directly across the street from Bill and Gayle Newman and their two boys, about 20' northeast from close assassination witnesses Jean Hill, and Mary Moorman as the limousine rounded the 120-degree slow turn from Houston Street onto Elm Street. The movie filming "babushka lady" was standing nearby to Brehm's right backside.

Brehm said President Kennedy was approaching him and only 30' away when his son then started to wave to President Kennedy, and the President started to wave back, then Brehm heard the first shot he remembered hearing. President Kennedy did not start waving until Zapruder film frame Z-171, which was after live oak tree branches and foliage had already temporarily hidden the President from Z-162 to Z-208 from being seen by anyone in the Texas School Book Depository's sixth-floor window.

Brehm stated to the FBI that "he could see the President's face very well, the President was seated, but was leaning forward when he stiffened perceptibly" and "seemed to stiffen and come to a pause" when the first shot Brehm remembered hearing was also the first shot that impacted the President and the President reacted immediately to being impacted.

When the President was 15' to 25' away, and had just passed, Brehm remembered hearing a second shot that struck President Kennedy in the head. Brehm watched the President's "hair fly up," "ripple," and "bits of brain and bone went flying" and "then roll over to his side" then President Kennedy "slumped all the way down."

The location of Brehm's November 22, 1963 written Dallas police voluntary affidavit statement is currently unknown.

In the 1966 video documentary *Rush to Judgment* while speaking of the blood cloud and the bits of brain and bone matter that Brehm saw flying in the air when the President's head exploded, Brehm stated he was specifically attracted to watch a piece fly towards himself, "over in the area of the curb where I was standing." ... "It seemed to have come left, and back." ... "Sir, whatever it was that I saw did fall, both, in that direction, and, over into the curb there."

Charles Brehm was located behind, and to the President's left when the President's head first exploded.

On November 22, 1963 only minutes after the assassination, and while still standing within Dealey Plaza, Brehm was quoted by a newspaper reporter as saying that Brehm, "seemed to think the shots came from in front of, or, beside the President."

In his November 24, 1963 FBI statement, and, during the 1987 Showtime cable-tv mock trial, *The Trial of Lee Harvey Oswald*, Brehm testified that the shots came from either the Texas School Book Depository or the Dal-Tex building.

In 1988, Brehm told author Larry Sneed, "After the car passed the building coming toward us, I heard a . . . surprising noise, and (the President) reached with both hands up to the side of his throat and kind of stiffened out . . . And when he got down in the area just past me, the second shot hit which damaged, considerably damaged, the top of his head. . . . That car took off in an evasive motion . . . and was just beyond me when a third shot went off. The third shot really frightened me! It had a completely different sound to it because it had really passed me as anybody knows who has been in down under targets in the Army or been shot at like I had been many times. You know when a bullet passes over you, the cracking sound it makes, and that bullet had an absolute crack to it. I do believe that that (third) shot was wild. It didn't hit anybody. I don't think it could have hit anybody. But it was a frightening thing to me because here was one shot that hit him, obviously; here was another shot that destroyed his head, and what was the reason for that third shot? That third shot frightened me more than the other two, and I grabbed the boy and threw him on the ground because I didn't know if we were going to have a 'shoot-'em-up' in this area."

Just like many other supporting witnesses, Brehm stated he distinctly remembered hearing another separate shot after the President's head had already exploded that missed hitting anyone, and that was the specific reason that Brehm immediately dragged his young son to the ground and covered him protectively.

Charles Brehm was not called to testify publicly in front of the Warren Commission, but he did supply a deposition.

Source (edited): "http://en.wikipedia.org/wiki/Charles_Brehm"

Clint Hill

For the football player of the same name, see Clint Hill (footballer)

Clinton J. Hill (born 1932) is a former United States Secret Service agent who was in the presidential motorcade during the assassination of John F. Kennedy. After Kennedy was shot, Hill ran from the car immediately behind the presidential limousine and leapt onto the back of it, holding on while the car raced to Parkland Memorial Hospital. This action was documented in the famous Zapruder film. Hill is the last surviving passenger of the presidential limousine which arrived at Parkland.

Hill was assigned to the Denver office of Secret Service in 1958. After John F. Kennedy was elected President of the United States, Hill was assigned to protect the First Lady, Jacqueline Kennedy. Hill became a nationally-known figure upon the assassination of President Kennedy on November 22, 1963.

Hill remained assigned to Mrs. Kennedy and the children until after the 1964 presidential election. He then was assigned to President Lyndon B. Johnson at the White House. In 1967, when Johnson was still in office, he became the Special Agent in Charge (SAIC) of Presidential protection. When Richard Nixon came into office, he moved over to SAIC of protection of Vice President Spiro Agnew. Finally, Hill was assigned to headquarters as the Assistant Director of the Secret Service for all protection. He retired in 1975.

The Kennedy assassination

President Kennedy was assassinated in Dallas, Texas, during a motorcade through the city while en route to a luncheon at the Dallas Trade Mart. The President and Mrs. Kennedy were riding in an open limousine containing three rows of seats. The Kennedys were in the rear seat of the car, and the Governor of Texas, John Connally, and his wife, Nellie Connally, were in the middle row. Secret Service agent William Greer was driving and the president's bodyguard, Roy Kellerman, was also in the front seat.

Clint Hill jumping on the presidential limousine, as captured on the Zapruder film.

Hill was riding in the car that was immediately behind the presidential limousine. As soon as the shooting began, Hill jumped out and began running to overtake the moving car in front of him with the plan to climb on from the rear bumper and crawl over the trunk to the back seat where the President and First Lady were located.

Hill grabbed a small handrail on the left rear of the trunk that was normally used by bodyguards to stabilize themselves while standing on small platforms on the rear bumper. According to the Warren Commission's findings there were no bodyguards stationed on the bumper that day because

...the President had frequently stated that he did not want agents to ride on these steps during a motorcade except when necessary. He had repeated this wish only a few days before, during his visit to Tampa, FL. .

The notion that the President's instructions in Tampa jeopardized his security in Dallas has since been denied by Hill and other agents. Regardless of Kennedy's statement photos taken of the motorcade along earlier segments of the route show Hill riding on the step at the back of the car.

As an alternate explanation fellow agent Gerald Blaine cites the location of the shooting:

We were going into a freeway, and that's where you take the speeds up to 60 and 70 miles an hour. So we would not have had any agents there anyway.

Hill grabbed the handrail less than two seconds after the fatal shot to the President. The driver then accelerated, causing the car to slip away from Hill, who was in the midst of trying to leap on to it. He succeeded in regaining his footing and jumped on to the back of the quickly accelerating vehicle.

As he got on, he saw Mrs. Kennedy, apparently in shock, crawling onto the flat rear trunk of the moving limousine (he later told the Warren Commission that he thought Mrs. Kennedy was reaching for a piece of the President's skull which had been blown off). Agent Hill crawled to her and guided the First Lady back into her seat. Once back in the car, Hill placed his body above the President and Mrs. Kennedy. Meanwhile, in the folding jump seats directly in front of them, Mrs. Connally had pulled her wounded husband, Governor John Connally, to a prone position on her lap.

Agent Kellerman, in the front seat of the car, gave orders over the car's two-way radio to the lead vehicle in the procession "To the nearest hospital, quick!" Hill was shouting as loudly as he could "To the hospital, to the hospital!" Enroute to the hospital, Hill flashed a "thumbs-down" signal and shook his head from side to side at the agents in the followup car, signaling the graveness of the President's condition.

As the car moved at high speed to the hospital, Hill maintained his position shielding the couple with his body, and was looking down at the mortally wounded President. Agent Hill later testified:

The right rear portion of his head was missing. It was lying in the rear seat of the car. His brain was exposed. There was blood and bits of brain all over the entire rear portion of the car.

Mrs. Kennedy was completely covered with blood. There was so much blood you could not tell if there had been any other wound or not, except for the one large gaping wound in the right rear portion of the head.

The limousine then rapidly exited Dealey Plaza and sped to Parkland Memorial Hospital, only minutes away, followed by other vehicles in the motorcade.

Although the Secret Service was shocked at its failure to protect the life of President Kennedy, virtually everyone agreed that Clint Hill's rapid and brave actions had been without blemish. He was honored at a ceremony in Washington just days after the funeral of John F. Kennedy. Mrs. Kennedy, despite being in deep mourning, made a rare appearance at this same event to personally thank him.

After the assassination

In a 1975 interview with Mike Wallace, Hill tearfully surmised that if he had reached the vehicle a second earlier, he would have been able to have taken the third shot to his own body, and felt a great deal of regret for not being able to reach there in time.

In popular culture

In the two-part *Quantum Leap* episode "Lee Harvey Oswald," Dr. Sam Beckett leapt out of Oswald and into Clint Hill. While this did not stop the President from being assassinated, in the "original" history, Oswald also assassinated Mrs. Kennedy, which Beckett/Hill prevented.

Source (edited): "http://en.wikipedia.org/wiki/Clint_Hill"

David Powers

David Francis Powers, Special Assistant to President John F. Kennedy.

David Francis Powers (April 25, 1912 – March 27, 1998) was Special Assistant and assistant Appointments Secretary to President of the United States John F. Kennedy. Powers served as Museum Curator of the John F. Kennedy Library and Museum from 1964 until his retirement in May 1994. Powers was a military veteran who had served in the U.S. Air Force during World War II from 1942 to 1945. Powers was also a very close, personal friend of John F. Kennedy.

During the assassination of President John F. Kennedy, Powers and Kenneth P. O'Donnell were riding in the Secret Service follow-up car directly behind the presidential limousine and are seen in the famous Zapruder film. Before the assassination, Powers had captured personal movie film footage showing the presidential limousine and Dallas crowds with his own movie camera until he ran out of film at 12:17 p.m., shortly before reaching Dealey Plaza. This film, now known as the "Powers film," was first made public in November 1996.

Powers and Kenneth O'Donnell co-authored *"Johnny We Hardly Knew Ye": Memories of John Fitzgerald Kennedy* (Boston: Little, Brown & Co., 1972). ISBN 0316716251

Powers' granddaughter, Jenny Powers, gained fame as a Broadway actress and performer. An ardent Democrat like her grandfather, she was asked to sing the National Anthem at the 2000 Democratic National Convention in Los Angeles.

Source (edited): "http://en.wikipedia.org/wiki/David_Powers"

Emmett Hudson

Emmett Joseph Hudson (21 May 1905, Arkansas – 23 June 1991, Dallas, Texas) was a witness to the assassination of U.S. President John F. Kennedy in Dallas, Texas, on 22 November 1963.

Hudson was employed by the Dallas Park Department as a groundskeeper in Dealey Plaza. As the Presidential motorcade drove through the plaza, Hudson was standing with two other men on a stairway on the grassy knoll north of Elm Street, about 33 feet (10 m) from the corner of a stockade fence atop the knoll. He heard a total of three shots, and said that the second shot was the one that hit the President in the head. He believed the shots came from the direction of the Texas School Book Depository. He testified to the Warren Commission that he saw no one with a gun except police officers.

Hudson was also interviewed for the House Select Committee on Assassinations in 1979, during which he confirmed his Warren Commission testimony, and said that he did not think that any shot was fired from behind the stockade fence.

Source (edited): "http://en.wikipedia.org/wiki/Emmett_Hudson"

Faye Chism

Marvin Faye Chism (born 1944) was a very close witness to the assassination of President John F. Kennedy within Dealey Plaza in Dallas Texas on November 22, 1963.

Faye, her husband, John, and their

3-year-old son, Ricky, were all standing together right up to Dealey Plaza's Elm Street north sidewalk curb, located at the eastern base of the grassy knoll. Chism was only 16' from President Kennedy at the closest point that he passed her during the assassination.

The Chism's were not filmed during the Zapruder film because they were hidden by the "Stemmons Freeway" sign, but, they are clearly visible in many other films, photos, and slide-photos captured before, during, and after the assassination.

Neither she nor her husband were ever called to testify publicly to the Warren Commission or the second assassination investigation by the House Select Committee on Assassinations.
Source (edited): "http://en.wikipedia.org/wiki/Faye_Chism"

George Jefferies

George Jefferies was born in 1925 in the United States. He was an amateur photographer who filmed home movie footage of John F. Kennedy, 90 seconds before he was assassinated.

The Footage
On November 22, 1963, Mr. Jefferies was in Dallas, Texas to see President John F. Kennedy in his motorcade. Using an 8mm camera, he took one of the best views of Mrs. Jackie Kennedy before the president was assassinated. Jefferies' film also shows Jackie's Secret Service bodyguard, Clint Hill, riding on the car's rear bumper for her protection. The footage is especially significant because it shows Kennedy's coat bunched up at his neck, a detail that appeased conspiracy theorists who have long questioned why the bullet hole in his body and coat had not matched up as expected.

Mr. Jefferies thought his footage was insignificant and kept it in a drawer for over 40 years until he mentioned it to his son-in-law, who in turn convinced him to donate it to the Sixth Floor Museum.
Source (edited): "http://en.wikipedia.org/wiki/George_Jefferies"

Gordon Arnold

Gordon L Arnold (August 14, 1943 – October 11, 1997, Dallas, Texas) is a man who claimed to have witnessed the assassination of U.S. President John F. Kennedy in Dallas, Texas.

Arnold served twelve years in the United States Army, after enlisting in 1963. After being discharged from the Army, Arnold married in 1966 (one living son as of 2004) and became employed with the Dallas Department of Consumer Affairs in Dallas, Texas.

In 1978 Arnold first publicly claimed to have been a witness to the 1963 assassination of John F. Kennedy in Dealey Plaza in Dallas. He claimed that minutes before the assassination he was twice approached by a business-suited CIA or Secret Service agent who demanded that he move from behind the picket fence of the Dealey Plaza north grassy knoll to the front of the fence. He claimed he moved just south of the picket fence and then filmed the assassination with a movie camera from a few feet north of a 3.3-foot (1 meter) high concrete retaining wall on the grassy knoll, and that a bullet passed extremely close to his left ear, then he dove to the ground. Arnold said that very soon after the end of the attack a man armed with a revolver and dressed in a Dallas police uniform kicked him while Arnold was still lying on the ground then demanded his movie film while another man armed with a rifle and also dressed in a Dallas police uniform and wearing yellow lens tinted "shooter's glasses" stood close by crying, shaking, and waving his rifle around. Arnold claimed he gave the revolver-armed police officer his movie camera, the police officer removed the film, then returned the camera to Arnold (now with the policeman's fresh fingerprints).

Arnold said that three days later he reported for his pre-assassination-scheduled transfer to the U.S. Army's Fort Wainwright in Alaska.

Despite his claims being made public some five months before the House Select Committee on Assassinations investigation ended, the HSCA, which did learn of his claims, decided not to interview him.

After 1978, Arnold provided his claims to only a few assassination researchers. Arnold has not been found in any of the photographs or films of the assassination and no witnesses report seeing him, including Abraham Zapruder or his assistant Marilyn Sitzman, who were very near where Arnold claimed to be that day, or seeing his alleged confrontation with two police officers, one crying and waving a rifle, on the grassy knoll moments after the assassination. Nor in any of his accounts did Arnold mention a young black couple whom Sitzman reported were sitting on a bench behind the same retaining wall where Arnold claimed to have been. Some researchers claim to have photographically enhanced his U.S. Army uniformed image in a Polaroid photograph taken by Mary Moorman during the assassination, while others claim this is actually the theorized "Badge Man" or simply just a tree or shadow.

Arnold elaborated on his claims in the 1988 documentary *The Men Who Killed Kennedy* and in a 1989 interview with the Sixth Floor Museum at Dealey Plaza. The transcript of that 1989 interview was eventually made available to the public in 2004.
Source (edited): "http://en.wikipedia.org/wiki/Gordon_Arnold"

Howard Brennan

Howard Brennan sitting across from the Texas School Book Depository in Dallas. Circle "A" indicates where he saw a man fire a rifle shot at President Kennedy's motorcade.

Howard Leslie Brennan (March 20, 1919 – December 22, 1983) was a witness to the assassination of U.S. President John F. Kennedy in Dallas, Texas on November 22, 1963. His description of a sniper he saw was, according to the Warren Commission, probative in reaching the conclusion that the shots came from the sixth floor, southeast corner window of the Texas School Book Depository Building.

The assassination

Brennan, a 44-year-old steamfitter, watched the presidential motorcade from a concrete retaining wall at the southwest corner of Elm and Houston streets in Dealey Plaza, where he had a clear view of the south side of the Depository Building. He arrived at about 12:23 p.m., and while waiting for the motorcade, he looked up and saw a man appear at an open window at the southeast corner of the sixth floor, 120 feet (37 m) from Brennan, and observed him leave the window "a couple of times."

Brennan watched the Presidential limousine turn left from Houston to Elm at 12:30, where it passed the Depository and headed toward a freeway entrance. Soon after the President's car passed, he heard an explosion like the backfire of a motorcycle.

" Well, then something, just right after this explosion, made me think that it was a firecracker being thrown from the Texas Book Store. And I glanced up. And this man that I saw previous was aiming for his last shot. . . . Well, as it appeared to me he was standing up. and resting against the left window sill, with gun shouldered to his right shoulder, holding the gun with his left hand and taking positive aim and fired his last shot. As I calculate a couple of seconds. He drew the gun back from the window as though he was drawing it back to his side and maybe paused for another second as though to assure himself that he hit his mark, and then he disappeared. "

Brennan quickly reported his observations to police officers, and a description of the suspect was broadcast to all Dallas police at 12:45 p.m., 12:48 p.m., and 12:55 p.m. About a half hour later, Patrolman J. D. Tippit was shot and killed, allegedly by Lee Harvey Oswald after Tippit spotted him walking along a sidewalk, and stopped to speak to him. Oswald fled and was captured in a nearby movie theater.

A few hours later, Brennan saw Oswald on television. Later the same evening Brennan identified Oswald in a police lineup as the person who most closely resembled the man in the window but Brennan said he was unable to make a positive identification. On December 17, 1963, he told the FBI that he was sure that Oswald was the rifleman he had seen in the window. Several months later, he also testified to the Warren Commission that at the time of the lineup, he believed the assassination was part of a conspiracy, and he was afraid for the safety of himself and his family. Because Brennan declined to make a positive identification in the police lineup, the commission regarded Brennan's subsequent testimony, that he sincerely believed he saw Oswald, as probative but not conclusive evidence that Oswald was the gunman in the sixth floor window.

The House Select Committee on Assassinations cited Howard Brennan in 1979 as support for its conclusion that the assassin shot at President Kennedy from the Book Depository Building.

Brennan's memoir *Eyewitness to History: The Kennedy Assassination as Seen by Howard L. Brennan*, written with J. Edward Cherryholmes, was published posthumously in 1987 by Texian Press. (ISBN 0872440761)
Source (edited): "http://en.wikipedia.org/wiki/Howard_Brennan"

Hurchel Jacks

Hurchel D. Jacks (1929-1995) was a Texas state trooper who guarded and drove Vice President Lyndon Johnson in the presidential motorcade on November 22, 1963 the day U.S. President John F. Kennedy was assassinated. The investigation of the assassination was conducted by the Warren Commission.

He joined the Texas Department of Public Safety in 1956 and retired as a DPS corporal in 1991.

He was often called on to escort VIPs during his career. "His life was very different from the ordinary highway patrolman's life," said his wife Bobby Jacks. "He met dignitaries, governors, and movie stars. He was pleased with that, but he never thought it was any great big deal."
Source (edited): "http://en.wikipedia.org/wiki/Hurchel_Jacks"

Ike Altgens

Altgens photograph taken during the assassination of John F. Kennedy. Kennedy is seen behind the rear-view mirror with his hands near his throat, and with Jackie Kennedy's gloved hand on his left arm; behind the limousine is the Texas School Book Depository.

James William "Ike" Altgens (April 28, 1919 – December 12, 1995) was an American photographer and field reporter for the Associated Press. Based in Dallas, Texas, in 1963, Altgens took arguably the most famous photograph of the in-progress assassination of President John F. Kennedy—a snapshot that led to a years-long debate among researchers over whether accused assassin Lee Harvey Oswald is visible in Dealey Plaza as the shots were fired.

Altgens spent more than 40 years with the AP, then did advertising work until he retired altogether. Both Altgens and his wife were in their seventies when they died in 1995, at about the same time, in their Dallas home.

Early life

Ike Altgens in the 1960s

Dallas native Ike Altgens was orphaned at a very young age and was raised by an aunt. In 1938, shortly after his graduation from North Dallas High School, he was hired by the Associated Press. The 19-year-old began his career by doing odd jobs and writing the occasional sports story; by 1940, he had demonstrated an aptitude for photography and was assigned to work in the wirephoto office.

His career was interrupted when he served in the United States Coast Guard during World War II; still, he managed to moonlight as a radio broadcaster. Following his return to Dallas, he married Clara B. Halliburton in July 1944, and returned to work with the AP the following year. He also attended night classes at Southern Methodist University, earning a Bachelor of Arts degree in speech with a minor in journalism.

By 1959, Altgens had enjoyed some success as an actor and model in television and print advertising. He portrayed the US Secretary of State in the low-budget film *Beyond the Time Barrier*, uttering its final line of dialogue: "That's a lot to think about!"

JFK assassination

Altgens had been employed by the AP for nearly 26 years when he was assigned on November 22, 1963, to photograph the motorcade that would take President Kennedy from Love Field to the Dallas Trade Mart, where Kennedy was scheduled to deliver an address. Working that day as the photo editor, Altgens asked instead to go to the railroad overcrossing known to locals as the "triple overpass" or "triple underpass" (where Elm, Main and Commerce Streets converge) to take pictures. Since that was not originally his assignment, Altgens took his personal camera, a 35 mm Nikkorex-F single-lens-reflex camera with a 105 mm telephoto lens, rather than the motor-driven camera usually used for news events. "This meant that what I took, I had to make sure it was good—I didn't have time for second chances."

Altgens later told investigators for the Warren Commission that he was denied access to the overcrossing by uniformed officers; he took up a position in Dealey Plaza instead. Though he took seven snapshots altogether, Altgens described to Commissioners only the photographs that were published; of those three, the first came as the Presidential limousine turned from Main Street onto Houston Street. Afterwards, he ran across the grass, roughly east to west, toward the south curb along Elm Street, and stopped across from the Plaza's north colonnade. As he snapped his first photograph from that spot, he heard a "burst of noise [that] he thought was firecrackers." Kennedy had just begun to react, thrusting his hands toward his throat; Jackie Kennedy's gloved left hand could be seen through the windshield, holding her husband's left arm.

Just as Altgens was preparing for a second snapshot along Elm Street, he heard a blast that he recognized as gunfire and saw the President had been struck in the head. "I had pre-focused, had my hand on the trigger, but when JFK's head exploded, sending substance in my direction, I virtually became paralyzed," Altgens later told author Richard B. Trask. "This was such a shock to me that I never did press the trigger on the camera.

Altgens' final photo taken just after the fatal shot shows Jackie Kennedy and Secret Service agent Clint Hill on the back of the Presidential limousine.

"[T]o have a President shot to death right in front of you," Altgens continued, "and keep your cool and do what you're supposed to do—I'm not real sure that the most seasoned photographers would be able to do it." Still, he said, "there is no excuse for this. I should have made the picture that I was set up to make. And I didn't do it."

Seconds later, Altgens had recovered enough to take his final picture of the limousine—showing the First Lady on the vehicle's trunk as Secret Service agent Clint Hill was climbing on behind her—as the driver had begun to speed away toward Parkland Memorial Hospital. Hill later told the Warren Commission that Jackie Kennedy appeared to be "reaching for something coming off the right rear bumper" of the limousine—described later as pieces of her husband's head—though Mrs. Kennedy's testimony suggested that she saw Altgens' photograph (or the corresponding still picture made from the Zapruder film) showing "me climbing out the back. But I don't remember that at all."

Very interestingly, Altgens (standing to President Kennedy's left and front when his head first exploded) stated during his Warren Commission testimony, "I wasn't keeping track of the number of pops that took place, but I could vouch for number one, and I can vouch for the last shot, but I cannot tell you how many shots were in between." Altgens further stated to author Richard Trask (in Trask's book, "Pictures of the Pain") that pieces of President Kennedy's head landed near his feet. Altgens also stated to attorney and author Mark Lane (in Lane's best selling book, "Rush to Judgment") that shortly before the limousine arrived inside the Dealey Plaza kill zone, Altgens observed several persons arrive up into the grassy knoll near the picket fence, and that one of these persons that Altgens distinctly observed was dressed in a uniform as a Dallas policeman: No policeman was, ever, officially ordered before, nor pre-stationed before, nor admitted to afterwards as, ever, being stationed near or on the grassy knoll.

Altgens testified that after the shots ended he followed officers and spectators up the grassy knoll on the north side of Elm Street. "I wanted to come over and get a picture of the guy—if they had such a person in custody." When they came back without a suspect, Altgens then ran to a telephone to report the shooting, and hurried back to the AP offices in the Dallas News Building on Houston Street to file his report and develop the film. His first phone call, from the AP wirephoto office to the news office, led to one of the first bulletins sent to the world:

Dallas, Nov. 22 (AP)— President Kennedy was shot today just as his motorcade left downtown Dallas. Mrs. Kennedy jumped up and grabbed Mr. Kennedy. She cried, 'Oh, no!' The motorcade sped on.

Controversial photograph

Of the three Altgens photos published by the Associated Press, the first snapped along Elm Street would receive the most scrutiny: taken simultaneously with Zapruder film frame 255 from the front and to the left of the Presidential limousine after Altgens had briefly walked out into the southernmost street lane while the shots were still being fired. Kennedy can be seen with his arms akimbo and his hands near his throat, apparently reacting to a shot fired by an assassin. Secret Service agents in the car immediately behind the limousine reacted differently to the sound; at least three are looking towards the President, one is facing the onlookers on the north side of Elm Street, and two are looking behind themselves, to their right-rear.

The man in the doorway (see image at top)

Several people can be seen standing in the main doorway to the Depository; one man bore a striking resemblance to Oswald. His presence there should have been impossible because, according to official investigations, he was on the building's sixth floor, firing bullets at Kennedy from a Mannlicher-Carcano rifle (Oswald claimed he was in the second-floor lunchroom, where he was spotted moments later by a Dallas Police officer). The Warren Commission paid careful attention to the image, as did private researchers: if the man was not Oswald, it did not necessarily prove nor disprove that Oswald was the assassin; if, however, the man *was* Oswald, here was photographic proof that he did not kill Kennedy.

A second Depository employee, Billy Lovelady, identified himself standing in the picture, and other employees who had been nearby agreed; a supervisor, however, signed an affidavit stating that Lovelady was "seated on the entrance steps". Ultimately, the Commission decided that Oswald was not in the doorway. That conclusion was bolstered several years later when photographs taken by a researcher of Lovelady, wearing what he said was the same shirt, appeared to match the image in the Altgens photograph (Oswald—who also claimed to have been outside having lunch with his supervisor, according to a police Captain's notes written "several days" after the interrogation—had been photographed wearing a similar shirt inside the Dallas Police station). In 1979, the House Select Committee on Assassinations also identified Lovelady after studying an enhanced version of the Altgens photograph and several amateur films. If that didn't clinch it, there is the famous newsreel film of Oswald being escorted down the hallway in Dallas Police headquarters. Asked whether he was in the "building" (the Depository) at the time of the shooting he replied "I work in that building. . . . Naturally if I work in that building, yes sir." Ten years later, Texas journalist Jim Marrs wrote, "[m]ost researchers today are ready to concede that the man may have been Lovelady."

Also of note in Altgen's famous image is the Dal-Tex Building, visible with its white fire escape in the far background of the photo. At least one of the prominent JFK conspiracy theories suggest there was a gunman in this building and/or on its roof, which, as can clearly be seen in this photograph, afforded an unobstructed view of the president's motorcade.

Later life

Altgens retired from the AP in 1979 after more than 40 years, rather than accept a transfer to a different bureau. He spent his later years working on display advertising for the Ford Motor Company, and was often contacted for interviews by assassination researchers who found him "polite and affable". Through all the telephone calls and letters, no one ever convinced him that the Warren Commission's conclusion—that Oswald, acting alone, killed Kennedy—could be wrong. "Until those people come up with solid evidence to support their claims," he told Trask, "I see no value in wasting my time with them." Still, he conceded, "there will always be some controversy about details surrounding the site and shooting of the President."

Oliver Stone's 1991 film *JFK* rekindled that controversy by reenacting the assassination, in Dealey Plaza, using actors as the victims and witnesses. Altgens was portrayed by Dallas-area actor John Depew.

By 1995, both Altgens and his wife were in declining health; their nephew, Dallas attorney Ron Grant, told the *Houston Chronicle* that his Aunt Clara "had been very ill for some time with heart trouble and many other problems. Both of them had had the flu for some time." On December 12, Ike and Clara Altgens were found dead in separate rooms in their home in Dallas. In addition to their failing health, police believed carbon monoxide poisoning from a faulty furnace might have played a role in their deaths. "With Mr. Altgens' passing," researcher Brad Parker wrote, "not only did history lose another witness, but many of us lost a valued friend."

Source (edited): "http://en.wikipedia.org/wiki/Ike_Altgens"

Jack Valenti

Jack Joseph Valenti (September 5, 1921 – April 26, 2007) was a long-time president of the Motion Picture Association of America. During his 38-year tenure in the MPAA, he created the MPAA film rating system, and he was generally regarded to have great cheeks and also as one of the most influential pro-copyright lobbyists in the world.

Early life

Valenti was born in Houston, Texas, USA, on September 5, 1921, the son of Italian immigrants. During World War II, he was a lieutenant in the United States Army Air Corps, flew 51 combat missions as the pilot-commander of a B-25 medium bomber and received four decorations.

Valenti was an alumnus of the University of Houston where he was awarded a B.B.A. in 1946. He later received an M.B.A. from Harvard University. During his time at UH, Valenti worked on *The Daily Cougar* newspaper staff, and served as president of the university's student government. Valenti would later serve on the university's board of regents, and became the School of Communication's namesake when it was renamed to the Jack J. Valenti School of Communication in April 2008. In 2002, the university also awarded him an honorary doctorate.

In 1952, he co-founded "Weekley & Valenti", an advertising/political consulting agency.

Political career

Valenti (far left) was present at Lyndon B. Johnson's swearing in aboard Air Force One.

Valenti's agency was in charge of the press during the November 1963 visit of President John F. Kennedy and Vice-President Lyndon B. Johnson to Dallas, Texas. Following the assassination of President Kennedy, Valenti was present in the famous photograph of Lyndon Johnson's swearing in aboard Air Force One, and rode with the new president to Washington. He then became the first "special assistant" to Johnson's White House and lived in the White House for the first two months of Johnson's presidency. In 1964, Johnson gave Valenti the responsibility to handle relations with the Republican Congressional leadership, particularly Gerald Ford and Charles Halleck from the House and Senator Everett Dirksen.

Valenti "loved LBJ as no serf ever adored his liege"; according to *The American Spectator*, "One old jibe has it that Valenti, a man who has kept the cowboy-bootlicking faith longer than anyone but Lady Bird and Bill Moyers, would have spun LBJ dropping the hydrogen bomb as an 'urban renewal project'." Valenti later called Johnson "the most single dominating human being that I've ever been in contact with" and "the single most intelligent man I've ever known."

Career in the MPAA

In 1966, Valenti, at the insistence of Universal Studios chief Lew Wasserman, and with Johnson's consent, resigned his White House commission and became the president of the Motion Picture Association of America. With Valenti's arrival in Hollywood, the pair were life-long allies, and together orchestrated and controlled how Hollywood would conduct business for the next several decades.

William Patry, a copyright attorney for the Clinton administration, who observed Valenti at first hand says:
His personal passion and extreme comfort around politicians gave him credibility that others ... would lack. Mr Valenti was a consummate salesman, who like all great salesmen ... worked himself up into believing the truth of his clients' message. Those privileged to see Mr Valenti offstage – talking openly with his clients about what could or could not be achieved, and what artifice would or would not work – are aware that Mr Valenti's clients frequently disagreed with his advice and directed him to deliver a different message through a different artifice. [He] was a great actor working on the stage of Washington DC (and sometimes globally) on behalf of an industry that appreciated his craft, but that never let him forget that the message was theirs and not his.

Movie rating system

In 1968, Valenti created the MPAA film rating system. The system initially comprised four distinct ratings: G, M, R, and X. The M rating would soon be replaced by GP, which was later changed to PG. The X rating immediately proved troublesome, since it was not trademarked and therefore was used freely by the pornography industry, with which it became most associated. Films such as *Midnight Cowboy* and *A Clockwork Orange* were assumed to be pornographic because they carried the X rating. In 1990 the NC-17 rating was introduced as a trademarked "adults only" replacement for the non-trademarked X-rating. The PG-13 rating was added in 1984 to provide a greater range of distinction for audiences.

Valenti on new technologies

During the late 1970s and early 1980s, Valenti became notorious for his colorful attacks on the Sony Betamax Video Cassette Recorder (VCR), which the MPAA feared would devastate the movie industry. He famously told a congressional panel in 1982, "I say to you that the VCR is to the American film producer and the American public as the Boston strangler is to the woman home alone." Despite Valenti's prediction, the home video market ultimately came to be the mainstay of movie studio revenues throughout the 1980s and 1990s.

Digital Millennium Copyright Act

Jack Valenti (1991)

In 1998 Valenti lobbied for the controversial Digital Millennium Copyright Act, arguing that copyright infringement via the Internet would severely damage the record and movie industries.

2003 screener ban injunction

In 2003, Valenti found himself at the center of the so-called screener debate, as the MPAA barred studios and many independent producers from sending screener copies of their films to critics and voters in various awards shows. Under mounting industry pressure and a court injunction *Antidote Int'l Films Inc. et al. v MPAA* (November 2003), Valenti backed down in 2004, narrowly avoiding a massive and embarrassing antitrust lawsuit against the MPAA.

The Coalition of Independent Filmmakers' Jeff Levy-Hinte, IFP/Los Angeles executive director Dawn Hudson and IFP/New York executive director Michelle Byrd said in a joint statement, "By obtaining a court order to force the MPAA to lift the screener ban last December, the Coalition enabled individual distributors to determine when and in what manner to distribute promotional screeners." It was viewed as Valenti's greatest professional loss.

Retirement

Valenti's salary in 2004 was reported to be $1.35 million, which made him the seventh-highest paid Washington trade group chief, according to the National Journal.

Valenti was nominated for President of the United States by the Alfalfa Club in 2004.

In August 2004, Valenti, then 82 years old, retired and was replaced by former U.S. Congressman, and Secretary of Agriculture, Dan Glickman. The current head of the ratings system, Joan Graves, was appointed by Valenti.

Post retirement he had become involved in technology-related venture capital activities, most recently joining the Advisory Board of Legend Ventures, where he advised on media investment opportunities. He also remained a supporter of causes linked to his Italian American heritage and was a member of the National Italian American Foundation (NIAF) for more than 20 years.

After retiring from the MPAA in 2004, Valenti became the first President of Friends of the Global Fight Against AIDS, Tuberculosis, and Malaria, an organization founded by philanthropists Edward W. Scott and Adam Waldman. The founders wanted to support the Global Fund to Fight AIDS, Tuberculosis and Malaria in its work to prevent millions of people from dying of preventable and treatable diseases each year. Under Mr. Valenti's leadership, Friends of the Global Fight oversaw a steady increase in U.S. funding for the Global Fund, resulting in a large-scale, positive impact in the fight against AIDS, tuberculosis and malaria. Valenti remained President of Friends of the Global Fight until his death in 2007.

Death

He died on April 26, 2007 at his home in Washington from stroke complications. He is buried at Arlington National Cemetery under a veteran's gravestone, which lists both his war decorations and his years as president of the MPAA.

Following his death, the National Italian American Foundation (NIAF) launched the NIAF Jack Valenti Institute, which provides support to Italian

American film students, in his memory. Director Martin Scorsese launched the institute at the Foundation's 32nd Anniversary Gala, after receiving an award from Mary Margaret Valenti.

Legacy

His memoirs *This Time, This Place: My Life in War, the White House and Hollywood* were published on May 15, 2007, only a few weeks after his death.

Honors

In 1969, Jack Valenti received the Bronze Medallion, New York City's highest civilian honor. In 1985, Jack Valenti received the French Légion d'Honneur.

In December 2003, Valenti received the "Legend in Leadership Award" from the Chief Executive Leadership Institute of the Yale School of Management.

In June 2005, the Washington DC headquarters of the Motion Picture Association of America, was renamed the Jack Valenti Building. It is located at 888 16th St. NW, Washington DC, very close to the White House. Jack Valenti maintained an office on the 8th floor, outside the MPAA's space, until his death.

In April 2008, the University of Houston renamed its School of Communication to the Jack J. Valenti School of Communication in his honor. Valenti was one of the school's notable alumni.

Personal life

Valenti had been a long-time bachelor until, in 1962, at the age of 41, he married Mary Margaret Valenti. They had three children: John, Alexandra and Warner Bros. studio executive Courtenay Valenti. He died just before their forty-fifth wedding anniversary.

In 1964, the FBI conducted an investigation concerning whether Valenti had a sexual relationship with a male photographer. The investigation concluded that there was no evidence that Valenti was a homosexual.

Books by Jack Valenti

- *Ten Heroes and Two Heroines (1957)*
- *The Bitter Taste of Glory (1971)*
- *A Very Human President* (1976; ISBN 0-671-80834-6)
- *Protect and Defend* (1992; ISBN 0-385-41735-7)
- *Speak Up With Confidence* (2002; ISBN 0-7868-8750-8)
- *This Time This Place* (2007; ISBN 0307346641)

Source (edited): "http://en.wikipedia.org/wiki/Jack_Valenti"

Jacqueline Kennedy Onassis

Jacqueline Lee Bouvier "Jackie" Kennedy Onassis (July 28, 1929 – May 19, 1994) was the wife of the 35th President of the United States, John F. Kennedy, and served as First Lady of the United States during his presidency from 1961 until his assassination in 1963. Five years later she married Greek shipping magnate Aristotle Onassis; they remained married until his death in 1975. For the final two decades of her life, Jacqueline Kennedy Onassis had a successful career as a book editor. She is remembered for her contributions to the arts and preservation of historic architecture, her style, elegance, and grace. A fashion icon, her famous pink Chanel suit has become a symbol of her husband's assassination and one of the lasting images of the 1960s.

Early life

Jacqueline Lee Bouvier was born in Southampton, New York, to Wall Street stock broker John Vernou Bouvier III (also known as "Black Jack Bouvier") and Janet Norton Lee. Jacqueline had a younger sister, Caroline Lee (known as Lee), born in 1933. Her parents divorced in 1940 and her mother married Standard Oil heir Hugh D. Auchincloss, Jr. in 1942. Through Janet's second marriage, Jacqueline gained a half sister and a half brother, Janet and James Auchincloss.

Jacqueline Bouvier in 1935.

Her mother's family, the Lees, were of Irish descent, and her father descended from French and English ancestors. Her maternal great grandfather emigrated from Cork, Ireland and later became the Superintendent of the New York City Public Schools. Michel Bouvier, Jacqueline's paternal great-great-grandfather, was born in France and was a contemporary of Joseph Bonaparte and Stephen Girard. He was a Philadelphia-based cabinetmaker, carpenter, merchant and real estate speculator. Michel's wife, Louise Vernou was the daughter of John Vernou, a French émigré tobacconist and Elizabeth Clifford Lindsay, an American-born woman. Jacqueline's grandfather, John Vernou Bouvier Jr., fashioned a more noble ancestry for his family in his vanity family history book *Our Forebears*. Recent scholarship and the research done by Jacqueline's cousin, John H. Davis, in his book *The Bouviers: Portrait of an American Family*, have disproved most of these fantasy lineages.

She spent her early years in New York City and East Hampton, New York at the Bouvier family estate, "Lasata". Following their parents' divorce, Jacqueline and Lee divided their time between their mother's homes in McLean, Virginia and Newport, Rhode Island and their father's homes in New York City and Long Island. She attended the Chapin School in New York City.

At a very early age she became an enthusiastic equestrienne, and horse-riding remained a lifelong passion.

Education and young adulthood

Bouvier attended the Holton-Arms School, located in Bethesda, Maryland, from 1942 to 1944 and Miss Porter's School, located in Farmington, Connecticut, from 1944 to 1947.

When she made her society debut in 1947, Hearst columnist Igor Cassini dubbed her "debutante of the year'.

Beginning in 1947, Bouvier spent her first two years of college at Vassar College, located in Poughkeepsie, New York, and then spent her junior year in France – at the University of Grenoble, located in Grenoble, and the Sorbonne, located in Paris – in a study-abroad program through Smith College, located in Northampton, Massachusetts. Upon returning home to the U.S., she transferred to The George Washington University, located in Washington, D.C. , graduating in 1951 with a Bachelor of Arts degree in French literature. Bouvier's college graduation coincided with her sister's high school graduation, and the two spent the summer of 1951 on a trip through Europe. This trip was the subject of her only autobiographical book, *One Special Summer,* – co-authored with her sister, which is also the only one of her publications to feature her drawings.

Following her graduation, Bouvier was hired as "Inquiring Photographer" for *The Washington Times-Herald*. The position required her to pose witty questions to individuals chosen at random on the street and take their pictures to be published alongside selected quotations from their responses in the newspaper. During this time, she was engaged to a young stock broker, John Husted, for three months.

Kennedy marriage and family

Jacqueline Kennedy at Hammersmith Farm in Newport, Rhode Island on the day of her wedding, September 12, 1953.

Bouvier and then-U.S. Representative John Kennedy belonged to the same social circle and often attended the same functions. In May 1952, at a dinner party organized by mutual friends, they were formally introduced for the first time. The two began dating soon afterward, and their engagement was officially announced on June 25, 1953.

Bouvier married Kennedy on September 12, 1953, at St. Mary's Church in Newport, Rhode Island in a Mass celebrated by Boston's Archbishop Richard Cushing. An estimated 700 guests attended the ceremony and 1,200 attended the reception that followed at Hammersmith Farm.

The wedding cake was created by Plourde's Bakery in Fall River, Massachusetts. The wedding dress, now housed in the Kennedy Library in Boston, Massachusetts, and the dresses of her attendants were created by designer Ann Lowe of New York City.

The newlyweds honeymooned in Acapulco, Mexico, before settling in their new home in McLean, Virginia. Kennedy suffered a miscarriage in 1955 and gave birth to a stillborn baby girl in 1956. That same year, the couple sold their estate, Hickory Hill, to Robert Kennedy and his wife Ethel Skakel Kennedy, moving to a townhouse on N Street in Georgetown. Kennedy subsequently gave birth to a second daughter, Caroline, in 1957, and a son, John, in 1960, both via Caesarian section.

First Lady of the United States

Campaign for Presidency

Jacqueline Kennedy campaigning alongside her husband in Appleton, Wisconsin, in March 1960

On January 3, 1960, John Kennedy announced his candidacy for the Presidency and launched his nationwide campaign. Though she had initially intended to take an active role in the campaign, Kennedy learned that she was pregnant shortly after the beginning of the campaign. Due to her previous difficult pregnancies, Kennedy's doctor instructed her to stay at home. From Georgetown, Kennedy participated in her husband's campaign by answering letters, taping television commercials, giving televised and printed interviews, and writing a weekly syndicated newspaper column, "Campaign Wife." She made rare personal appearances.

As First Lady

First Lady Jacqueline Kennedy, President John F. Kennedy, André Malraux, Marie-Madeleine Lioux Malraux, Lyndon B. Johnson and Lady Bird Johnson having just descended White House Grand Staircase on their way to a dinner with the French cultural minister, April 1962. The First Lady wears a gown designed by Oleg Cassini.

In the general election on November 8, 1960, John F. Kennedy narrowly beat Republican Richard Nixon in the U.S. presidential election. A little over two weeks later, Jacqueline Kennedy gave birth to the couple's first son, John, Jr. When her husband was sworn in as president on January 20, 1961, Kennedy became, at age 31, one of the youngest First Ladies in history, behind Frances Folsom Cleveland and Julia Tyler.

Like any First Lady, Kennedy was thrust into the spotlight and while she did not mind giving interviews or being photographed, she preferred to maintain as much privacy as possible for herself and her children.

Kennedy is remembered for reorganizing entertainment for White House social events, restoring the interior of the presidential home, her taste in clothing worn during her husband's presidency, her popularity among foreign dignitaries, and leading the country in mourning after JFK's 1963 assassination.

Kennedy ranks among the most popular of First Ladies.

Social success

As First Lady, Kennedy devoted much of her time to planning social events at the White House and other state properties. She often invited artists, writers, scientists, poets, and musicians to mingle with politicians, diplomats, and statesmen.

Perhaps due to her skill at entertaining, Kennedy proved quite popular among international dignitaries. When Soviet Premier Nikita Khrushchev was asked to shake President Kennedy's hand for a photo, Khrushchev said, "I'd like to shake her hand first." Jacqueline was well received in Paris, France, when she visited with her husband, and when she traveled with Lee to Pakistan and India in 1962.

Mrs. Kennedy with Charles Collingwood on the broadcasted tour of the restored White House (1962).

White House restoration

The Blue Room of the White House as redecorated by Stéphane Boudin in 1962. Boudin chose the period of the Madison administration, returning much of the original French Empire style furniture.

The restoration of the White House was Kennedy's first major project as First Lady. She was dismayed during her pre-inauguration tour of the White House to find little of historic significance in the house. The rooms were furnished with undistinguished pieces that she felt lacked a sense of history. Her first efforts, begun her first day in residence (with the help of society decorator Sister Parish), were to make the family quarters attractive and suitable for family life. Among these changes was the addition of a kitchen on the family floor and rooms for her children. Upon almost immediately exhausting the funds appropriated for this effort, Kennedy established a fine arts committee to oversee and fund the restoration process and asked early American furniture expert Henry du Pont to consult.

While her initial management of the project was hardly noted at the time, later accounts have noted that she managed the conflicting agendas of Parish, du Pont, and Boudin with seamless success; she initiated publication of the first White House guidebook, whose sales further funded the restoration; she initiated a Congressional bill establishing that White House furnishings would be the property of the Smithsonian Institution, rather than available to departing ex-presidents to claim as their own; and she wrote personal requests to those who owned pieces of historical interest that might be, and later were, donated to the White House.

Jacqueline Kennedy in the diplomatic reception room of the White House

On February 14, 1962, Kennedy took American television viewers on a tour of the White House with Charles Collingwood of CBS News. In the tour she said, "I just feel that everything in the White House should be the best—the entertainment that's given here. If it's an American company you can help, I like to do that. If not—just as long as it's the best." Working with Rachel Lambert Mellon, she oversaw redesign and replanting of the White House Rose Garden and the East Garden, which was renamed the Jacqueline Kennedy Garden after her husband's assassination. Her efforts on behalf of restoration and preservation at the White House left a lasting legacy in the form of the White House Historical Association, the Committee for the Preservation of the White House which was based upon her White House Furnishings Committee, a permanent Curator of the White House, the White House Endowment Trust, and the White House Acquisition Trust.

Broadcasting of the White House restoration greatly helped the Kennedy administration. The U.S. government sought international support during the Cold War, which it achieved by affecting public opinion. The First Lady's celebrity and high profile status made viewing the tour of the White House very desirable. The tour was filmed and distributed to 106 countries since there was a great demand from the elite as well as people in power to see the film. In 1962 at the 14th Annual Emmy Awards (NBC, May 22), Bob Newhart emceed from the Hollywood Palladium; Johnny Carson from the New York Astor Hotel; and NBC newsman David Brinkley hosted at the Sheraton Park Hotel in Washington D.C., and took the spotlight as a special Academy of Television Arts and Sciences Trustees Award was given to Jacqueline Kennedy for her CBS-TV tour of the White House. Lady Bird Johnson accepted for the camera-shy First Lady. The Emmy statuette is on display in the Kennedy Library located in Boston, Massachusetts. Focus and admiration for Jacqueline Kennedy took negative attention away from her husband. By attracting worldwide public attention, the First Lady gained allies for the White House and international support for the Kennedy administration and its Cold War policies.

Foreign trips

Jacqueline Kennedy at the Taj Mahal, Agra, Uttar Pradesh, India on March 15, 1962.

Before the Kennedys visited France, a television special was shot in French with the First Lady on the White House lawn. After arriving in the country, she impressed the public with her ability to speak fluent French, as well as her extensive knowledge of its history. Jacqueline had been aided in her learning of the French language by the prominent Puerto Rican educator María Teresa Babín Cortés. At the conclusion of the visit, *Time* magazine seemed delighted with the First Lady and noted, "There was also that fellow who came with her." Even President Kennedy joked, "I am the man who accompanied Jacqueline Kennedy to Paris — and I have enjoyed it!"

Pakistani President Ayub Khan and Jacqueline Kennedy with Sardar (1962)

At the urging of John Kenneth Galbraith, U.S. Ambassador to India, she undertook a tour of India and Pakistan, taking her sister Lee Radziwill along with her, which was amply documented in photojournalism of the time as well as in Galbraith's journals and memoirs. At the time, Ambassador Galbraith noted a considerable disjunction between Kennedy's widely-noted concern with clothes and other frivolity and, on personal acquaintance, her considerable intellect.

While in Karachi, Pakistan, she found some time to take a ride on a camel with her sister. In Lahore, Pakistan, Pakistani President Ayub Khan presented the First Lady with a much-photographed horse, Sardar (the Urdu term meaning "leader"). Subsequently this gift was widely misattributed to the king of Saudi Arabia, including in the various recollections of the Kennedy White House years by President Kennedy's friend, journalist and editor Benjamin Bradlee. While at a reception in her honor at the Shalimar Gardens, Kennedy told guests "all my life I've dreamed of coming to the Shalimar Gardens. It's even lovelier than I'd dreamed. I only wish my husband could be with me."

Death of younger son

Early in 1963, Kennedy became pregnant again and curtailed her official duties. She spent most of the summer at the Kennedys' rented home on Squaw Island, near the Kennedy family's Cape Cod compound at Hyannis Port, where she went into premature labor on August 7, 1963. She gave birth to a boy, Patrick Bouvier Kennedy, via emergency Caesarian section at Otis Air Force Base, five and a half weeks prematurely. His lungs were not fully developed, and he died at Boston Children's Hospital of hyaline membrane disease (now known as respiratory distress syndrome) on August 9, 1963.

Assassination and funeral of John F. Kennedy

John & Jacqueline Kennedy at Love Field in Dallas on the day of the assassination

The Presidential limousine before the assassination. Jacqueline is in the back seat to the President's left.

Jackie wearing her blood-stained pink suit while Johnson took oath of office as president.

On November 21, 1963, the First Couple left the White House for a political trip to Texas, stopping in San Antonio, Houston, and Fort Worth that day. After a breakfast on November 22, the Kennedys flew from Fort Worth's Carswell Air Force Base to Dallas's Love Field on Air Force One, accompanied by Texas Governor John Connally and his wife Nellie. She was wearing a bright pink Chanel suit. A 9.5-mile (15.3 km) motorcade was to take them to the Trade Mart where the President was scheduled to speak at a lunch. The First Lady was seated next to her husband in the limousine, with the Governor and his wife seated in front of them. Vice President Johnson and his wife followed in another car in the motorcade.

After the motorcade turned the corner onto Elm Street in Dealey Plaza, the First Lady heard what she thought to be a motorcycle backfiring, and did not realize that it was a gunshot until she heard Governor Connally scream. Within 8.4 seconds, two more shots had rung out, and she leaned toward her husband. The final shot struck the President in the head. Shocked, she climbed out of the back seat and crawled over the trunk of the car. Her Secret Service agent, Clint Hill, later told the Warren Commission that he thought she had been reaching across the trunk for a piece of the President's skull that had been blown off. Hill ran to the car and leapt onto it, directing her back to her seat. The car rushed to Dallas's Parkland Hospital, and on arrival there, the president's body was rushed into a trauma room. The First Lady, for the moment, remained in a room for relatives and friends of patients just outside.

A few minutes into her husband's treatment, accompanied by the President's doctor, Admiral George Burkley, she left her folding chair outside Trauma Room One and attempted to enter the operating room. Nurse Doris Nelson stopped her and attempted to bar the door to prevent her from entering. She persisted, and the President's doctor suggested that she take a sedative, which she refused. "I want to be there when he dies," she told Burkley. He eventually persuaded Nelson to grant her access to Trauma Room One, saying "It's her right, it's her prerogative."

Later, when the casket arrived, the widow removed her wedding ring and slipped it onto the President's finger. She told aide Ken O'Donnell, "Now I have nothing left."

Family members depart the U.S. Capitol after a lying-in-state ceremony for the President, November 24, 1963.

After the president's death, she refused to remove her blood-stained clothing, and regretted having washed the blood off her face and hands. She continued to wear the blood-stained pink suit as she went on board Air Force One and stood next to Johnson when he took the oath of office as President. She told Lady Bird Johnson, "I want them to see what they have done to Jack."

Kennedy took an active role in planning the details of her husband's state funeral, which was based on Abraham Lincoln's. The funeral service was held at Cathedral of St. Matthew the Apostle, Washington D.C., and the burial at Arlington National Cemetery; the widow led the procession there on foot and would light the eternal flame at the grave site, a flame that had been created at her request. Lady Jeanne Campbell reported back to *The London Evening Standard*: "Jacqueline Kennedy has given the American people... one thing they have always lacked: Majesty."

Following the assassination and the media coverage which had focused intensely on her during and after the burial, Kennedy stepped back from official public view. She did, however, make a brief appearance in Washington to honor the Secret Service agent, Clint Hill, who had climbed aboard the limousine in Dallas to try to shield her and the President.

Life following the JFK assassination

Jackie Kennedy's Official White House Portrait by Aaron Shikler.

A week after the assassination, Jacqueline was interviewed in Hyannisport, Massachusetts, on November 29 by Theodore H. White of *Life* magazine. In that session, she compared the Kennedy years in the White House to King Arthur's mythical Camelot, commenting that the President often played the title song of Lerner and Loewe's musical recording before retiring to bed. She also quoted Queen Guinevere from the musical, trying to express how the loss felt.

Her steadiness and courage after her husband's assassination and funeral won her admiration around the world. Following his death, Kennedy and her children remained in their quarters in the White House for two weeks, preparing to vacate. They spent the winter of 1964 in Averell Harriman's home in the Georgetown section of Washington, D.C., before purchasing her own home on the same street. Later in 1964, in the hope of having more privacy for her children, Kennedy decided to buy an apartment on Fifth Avenue in New York City and sold her new Georgetown house and the country home in Atoka, Virginia, where she and her husband had intended to retire. She spent a year in mourning, making few public appearances; during this time, Caroline told one of her teachers that her mother cried frequently.

Kennedy perpetuated her husband's memory by attending selected memorial dedications. These included the 1967 christening of the U.S. Navy aircraft carrier USS *John F. Kennedy* (CV-67) (decommissioned in 2007), in Newport News, Virginia, and a memorial in Hyannisport. They also included the dedication of the United Kingdom's official memorial to President Kennedy at Runnymede, England, and the dedication of a park near New Ross, Ireland. She oversaw plans for the establishment of the John F. Kennedy Library, which is the repository for official papers of the Kennedy Administration. Original plans to have the library situated in Cambridge, Massachusetts, near Harvard University, proved problematic for various reasons, so it is situated in Boston. The finished library, designed by I.M. Pei, includes a museum and was dedicated in Boston in 1979 by President Jimmy Carter.

In November 1967, during the midst of the Vietnam War, *Life* magazine recognized Jacqueline as "America's unofficial roving ambassador" during her visit to Cambodia when she met with Chief of State Norodom Sihanouk. During the visit, Kennedy joined Sihanouk on a visit to Angkor Wat. At that point, diplomatic relations between the U.S. and Cambodia had been broken since May 1965.

Onassis marriage

In June 1968 when her brother-in-law Robert F. Kennedy was assassinated, she came to fear for her life and that of her children, saying "If they're killing Kennedys, then my children are targets...I want to get out of this country." On October 20, 1968, she married Aristotle Onassis, a wealthy, Greek shipping magnate, who was able to provide the privacy and security she needed for herself and her children.

The wedding took place on Skorpios, Onassis's private island in the Ionian Sea, Greece. After her marriage to Onassis, Jacqueline lost her Secret Service protection and her franking privilege, both of which are entitlements to a widow of U.S. president. As a result of the marriage, the media gave her the nickname "Jackie O", which remained a popular shorthand reference to her. She became the target of paparazzi who were following her.

Then tragedy struck again, as Aristotle Onassis's only son Alexander died in a plane crash in January 1973. Onassis's health began deteriorating rapidly and he died in Paris, on March 15, 1975. Jacqueline's financial legacy was severely limited under Greek law, which dictated how much a non-Greek surviving spouse could inherit. After two years of legal battle, she eventually accepted from Christina Onassis, Onassis's daughter and sole heir, a settlement of $26 million, waiving all other claims to the Onassis estate.

During their marriage, the couple resided in a home they rented in Bernardsville, New Jersey.

Later years

Onassis's death in 1975 made her, then nearly 46, a widow for the second time. Now that her children were older, she decided to find work that would be fulfilling to her. Since she had always enjoyed writing and literature, in 1975 Jacqueline accepted a job offer as an editor at Viking Press. But, in 1978, the President of Viking Press, Thomas H. Guinzburg, authorized the purchase of the Jeffrey Archer novel *Shall We Tell the President?*, which was set in a fictional future presidency of Edward M. Kennedy and described an assassination plot against him. Although Guinzburg cleared the book purchase and publication with Onassis, upon the publication of a negative *New York Times* review which asserted that Onassis held some responsibility for its publication, she abruptly resigned from Viking Press the next day. She then moved to Doubleday as an associate editor under an old friend, John Sargent, living in New York City, Martha's Vineyard and the Kennedy Compound in Hyannis, Massachusetts. From the mid 1970s until her death, her companion was Maurice Tempelsman, a Belgian-born industrialist and diamond merchant who was long separated from his wife.

She also continued to be the subject of much press attention, most notoriously involving the photographer Ron Galella. He followed her around and photographed her as she went about her day-to-day activities, obtaining candid, iconic photos of her. She ultimately obtained a restraining order against him and the situation brought attention to paparazzi-style photography. In 1995, John F. Kennedy Jr. allowed Galella to photograph him at public events.

Among the many books she edited was Larry Gonick's *The Cartoon History of the Universe*. He expressed his gratitude in the acknowledgments in Volume 2.

Former First Lady Jacqueline Kennedy Onassis in 1986 during a visit from the President and First Lady, Ronald and Nancy Reagan. Nancy Reagan was the first First Lady since Kennedy to be regarded as generally glamorous, and thus the two were sometimes compared

Jacqueline Onassis also appreciated the contributions of African-American writers to the American literary canon. She encouraged Dorothy West, her neighbor on Martha's Vineyard and the last surviving member of the Harlem Renaissance, to complete the novel *The Wedding* (1995), a multi-generational story about race, class, wealth, and power in the U.S.; West acknowledged Onassis's encouragement in the foreword. The novel, which received literary acclaim when it was published by Doubleday, was later adapted into a television miniseries of the same name (1998) starring Halle Berry.

She also worked to preserve and protect America's cultural heritage. The notable results of her hard work include Lafayette Square in Washington, D.C, and Grand Central Terminal, New York City's historic railroad station. While she was First Lady, she helped to stop the destruction of historic homes in Lafayette Square, because she felt that these buildings were an important part of the nation's capital and played an essential role in its history. Later, in New York City, she led a historic preservation campaign to save from demolition and renovate Grand Central Terminal. A plaque inside the terminal acknowledges her prominent role in its preservation. In the 1980s, she was a major figure in protests against a planned skyscraper at Columbus Circle which would have cast large shadows on Central Park; the project was cancelled, but a large twin towered skyscraper would later fill in that spot in 2003, the Time Warner Center.

From her apartment windows in New York City she had a splendid view of a glass enclosed wing of the Metropolitan Museum of Art which displays the Temple of Dendur. This was a gift from Egypt to the U.S. in gratitude for the generosity of the Kennedy administration, who had been instrumental in saving several temples and objects of Egyptian antiquity that would otherwise have been flooded after the construction of the Aswan Dam.

Death

In January 1994 Onassis was diagnosed with non-Hodgkin's lymphoma, a form of cancer. Her diagnosis was announced to the public the following month. The family and doctors were initially optimistic, and she stopped smoking at the insistence of her daughter, having previously been a three-pack-a-day smoker. Onassis continued her work with Doubleday, but curtailed her schedule. By April, the cancer had spread, and she made her last trip home from New York Hospital-Cornell Medical Center on May 18, 1994. A large crowd of well-wishers, tourists, and reporters gathered on the street outside her apartment. Onassis died in her sleep at 10:15 p.m. on Thursday, May 19, two and a half months before her 65th birthday. In announcing her death, Jacqueline's son, John Kennedy Jr., stated, "My mother died surrounded by her friends and her family and her books, and the people and the things that she loved. She did it in her own way, and on her own terms, and we all feel lucky for that."

Grave of Jacqueline Bouvier Kennedy Onassis at Arlington National Cemetery (2006)

Onassis' funeral was held on May 23 at Saint Ignatius Loyola Church in Manhattan — the church where she was baptized in 1929, and confirmed as a teenager. At her funeral, her son John described three of her attributes as the love of words, the bonds of home and family, and the spirit of adventure. She was buried alongside President Kennedy, their son Patrick, and their stillborn daughter Arabella at Arlington National Cemetery in Arlington, Virginia.

In her will, Onassis left her children Caroline and John an estate valued at $43.7 million by its executors.

Fashion icon

John & Jacqueline Kennedy watching America's Cup race on board the USS *Joseph P. Kennedy Jr.*, September 1962.

During her husband's presidency, Jacqueline Kennedy became a symbol of fashion for women all over the world. She retained French-born American fashion designer and Kennedy family friend Oleg Cassini in the fall of 1960 to create an original wardrobe for her as First Lady. From 1961 to late 1963, Cassini dressed her in many of her most iconic ensembles, including her Inauguration Day fawn coat and Inaugural gala gown as well as many outfits for her visits to Europe, India and Pakistan. In her first year in the White House, Kennedy spent $45,446 more on fashion than the $100,000 annual salary her husband earned as president. Her clean suits with a skirt hem down to middle of the knee, three-quarter sleeves on notch-collar jackets, sleeveless A-line dresses, above-the-elbow gloves, low-heel pumps, and famous pillbox hats were an overnight success around the world that quickly became known as the "Jackie" look. Although Cassini was her primary designer, she also wore ensembles by French fashion legends such as Chanel, Givenchy, and Dior. More than any other First Lady her style was copied by commercial manufacturers and a large segment of young women.

In the years after the White House, her style changed dramatically. Gone were the modest "campaign wife" clothes. Wide-leg pantsuits, large lapel jackets, gypsy skirts, silk Hermès head scarves and large, round, dark sunglasses were her new look. She often chose to wear brighter colors and patterns and even began wearing jeans in public. Beltless, white jeans with a black turtleneck, never tucked in, but pulled down over the hips, also was a fashion trend that she set.

Throughout her lifetime, Kennedy acquired a large collection of exquisite and priceless jewelry. Her triple-strand pearl necklace designed by American jeweler Kenneth Jay Lane became her signature piece of jewelry during her time as First Lady in the White House. Often referred to as the "berry brooch," the two fruit cluster brooch of strawberries made of rubies with stems and leaves of diamonds, designed by French jeweler Jean Schlumberger for Tiffany & Co., was personally selected and given to her by her husband several days prior to his inauguration in January 1961. Schlumberger's gold and enamel bracelets were worn by Kennedy so frequently in the early and mid-1960s that the press called them "Jackie bracelets". His white enamel and gold "banana" earrings were also favored by her. Kennedy wore jewelry designed by Van Cleef & Arpels throughout the 1950s, 1960s and 1970s. Her sentimental favorite was the wedding ring given to her by President Kennedy, also from Van Cleef & Arpels.

Honors and memorials

- A high school named Jacqueline Kennedy Onassis High School for International Careers, was dedicated by New York City in 1995, the first high school named in her honor. It is located at 120 West 46th Street between Sixth and Seventh Avenues, and was formerly the High School for the Performing Arts.
- In December 1999, Onassis was among 18 included in Gallup's List of Widely Admired People of the 20th Century, from a poll conducted of the American people.

A 2007 view across the Jacqueline Kennedy Onassis Reservoir in Central Park, located in New York City, New York. Joggers use the running path encircling the reservoir, located in the northern portion of the park.

- The main reservoir in Central Park, located in New York City, New York, was renamed in her honor as the Jacqueline Kennedy Onassis Reservoir.
- The Municipal Art Society of New York presents the Jacqueline Kennedy Onassis Medal to an individual whose work and deeds have made an outstanding contribution to the city of New York. The medal was named in honor of the former MAS board member in 1994, for her tireless efforts to preserve and protect New York City's great architecture.
- At George Washington University, a residence hall located on the southeast corner of I and 23rd streets NW in Washington, D.C., was renamed Jacqueline Bouvier Kennedy Onassis Hall in honor of the alumna.
- The White House's East Garden was renamed the Jacqueline Kennedy Garden in her honor.
- In 2007, her name and her first husband's were included on the list of people aboard the Japanese *Kaguya* mission to the moon launched on September 14, as part of The Planetary Society's "Wish Upon The Moon" campaign. In addition, they are included on the list aboard NASA's Lunar Reconnaissance Orbiter mission.
- A school and an award at the American Ballet Theatre have been named after her in honor of her childhood

study of ballet.
- The companion book for a series of interviews between mythologist Joseph Campbell and Bill Moyers, *The Power of Myth*, was created under the direction of Onassis, prior to her death. The book's editor, Betty Sue Flowers, writes in the *Editor's Note* to *The Power of Myth*: "I am grateful... to Jacqueline Lee Bouvier Kennedy Onassis, the Doubleday editor, whose interest in the books of Joseph Campbell was the prime mover in the publication of this book." A year after her death in 1994, Moyers dedicated the companion book for his PBS series, *The Language of Life* to Onassis. The dedication read: "To Jacqueline Kennedy Onassis. As you sail on to Ithaka." Ithaka was a reference to the C.P. Cavafy poem that Maurice Tempelsman read at her funeral.
- A white gazebo is dedicated to Jacqueline Kennedy Onassis on North Madison Street in Middleburg, Virginia. Jacqueline and President Kennedy frequented the small town of Middleburg and intended to retire in the nearby town of Atoka. She also hunted with the Middleburg Hunt numerous times.

Cultural depictions

Source (edited): "http://en.wikipedia.org/wiki/Jacqueline_Kennedy_Onassis"

James M. Chaney

James M. Chaney (July 24, 1921 – April 19, 1976) was a witness and Dallas police motorcycle presidential escort riding only ten to fifteen feet away from (slightly behind and to the right of) President John F. Kennedy during his assassination on November 22, 1963 within Dealey Plaza in Dallas, Texas. He is not to be confused with James E. Chaney, one of three civil rights workers murdered in Mississippi in 1964.

JFK's Assassination

In a November 22, 1963 interview with reporter Bill Lord recorded by Dallas ABC TV, Chaney stated he remembered hearing three shots. Chaney said when he heard the first shot he remembered that it sounded like a motorcycle backfiring and Chaney immediately looked to his left and saw President Kennedy had "looked back over his left shoulder" within the limousine. In the famous Ike Altgens photo taken concurrent with Zapruder film frame 255, Chaney is seen very close to the limousine facing President Kennedy. Chaney further stated that "the second shot hit him in the face," and that a third shot was fired that Chaney did not see hit the president but he did see Governor John B. Connally's shirt erupt in blood. Chaney stated that the shots he remembered hearing seemed to come from "back over my right shoulder." During the assassination his police uniform was spattered with blood and President Kennedy's head matter.

On November 23, 1963 Chaney was stationed on duty within Dealey Plaza and spoke with nightclub owner and alleged organized crime member Jack Ruby when Ruby stopped by the plaza to see the memorial wreaths, flowers, and messages placed there by mourners.

James Chaney, the closest non-limousine witness to the president during the assassination, was never called by the Warren Commission to testify.

Death

Chaney died a relatively young man in April, 1976 from his 2nd heart attack. He did not die during the House Select Committee on Assassinations investigation into the assassination which was formed in September 1976 as previously erroneously stated.

Source (edited): "http://en.wikipedia.org/wiki/James_M._Chaney"

James Tague

James "Jim" Thomas Tague (born October 17, 1936, Plainfield, Indiana) was a witness to the assassination of U. S. President John F. Kennedy in Dallas, Texas on November 22, 1963. He received a minor wound on his right cheek during the assassination. He is the only person, in addition to Kennedy and Texas Governor John B. Connally, known to have been wounded by gunfire in Dallas' Dealey Plaza that day.

The assassination

Tague had been driving to downtown Dallas to have lunch with a friend when he came upon a traffic jam due to the presidential motorcade. This caused him to stop his car, get out of it, and stand by Dealey Plaza, at the south curb of Main Street, 520 feet (158 m) southwest of the Texas School Book Depository. He was a few feet east of the eastern edge of the triple overpass railroad bridge, when Tague saw the Presidential limousine, and heard the first shot.

Like many other witnesses, Tague remembered hearing this first shot and likened it to a firecracker. Tague later testified that the first shot he recalled hearing occurred after the Presidential limousine had already completed the 120-degree slow turn from Houston Street onto Elm Street and then straightened out. The motorcade then proceeded towards him.

Soon after the shots were fired Tague was approached by a Dallas sheriff detective, Buddy Walthers, who had noticed that Tague had specks of blood on his right facial cheek. (Tague also had a small left facial scab, caused by an unrelated event which occurred a week prior to assassination) The detective asked Tague where he had been standing. The two men then examined the area and discovered — on the upper part of the Main Street south curb — a "very fresh scar" impact that, to each of them, looked like a bullet had struck there and taken a small chip out of the curb's concrete. They came to the conclusion that one bullet ricocheted off the curb and the debris hit Tague. This curb surrounding the scar chip was removed and replaced on Saturday November 23, 1963 (the day after the assassination) and is now in the National Archives. The scar chip was 23 feet 6 inches (7.2 m) east of the east edge of the Triple Underpass railroad bridge, about 20 (6.1 m) feet from where Tague stood during the attack. The detective told Tague it looked like a bullet had been fired from one of the Houston and Elm Streets intersection buildings and had hit the curb.

After the assassination

The Warren Commission and the FBI

Six months after the assassination, Tague was called to testify before the Warren Commission. When he gave his testimony, Tague initially stated that he was wounded on his facial cheek by either the second or third shot of the three shots that he remembered hearing. When the Commission counsel pressed him to be more specific, Tague testified that he was wounded by the second shot. When the Commission counsel asked Tague where he sensed was the source of the gun shots, Tague testified the shots originated "from the monument or whatever it was" which was the area of the North Pergola Monument, located on the grassy knoll, several hundred feet west of the Book Depository building.

Later, forensic tests by the FBI revealed that the chipped bullet mark impact location did not have any copper metal residue embedded in it. This strongly indicates that at the instant that the bullet or bullet fragment struck the curb, it did not have a military jacketed copper outer casing, such as those required by the 6.5 mm military jacketed copper encased bullets, allegedly, fired from the far eastern sixth floor window of the School Book Depository.

Sometime after being forensically examined by the FBI in 1964, the spectrographic slides containing the trace physical elements of the bullet embedded into the curb's chipped scar disappeared from the FBI evidence storage. The FBI later claimed (only after author/researcher/Congressional investigator Harold Weisberg filed a Freedom of Information Act lawsuit) that they had destroyed the spectrographic slides to save space within the FBI building.

1983 - 2003

A 1983 documented study of the curb scar, conducted by an engineering firm hired by the *Reader's Digest*, concluded that the curb scar had been covered over with a foreign material. A photograph of the curb taken by a FBI agent just before the curb stone was cut out of the street in August 1964 shows the curb had been patched before it was cut from the street. Tague, in his book *Truth Withheld*, has pictures of the scar taken on November 23, 1963, and as it sat in the National Archives in 1997. The photo taken on November 23, 1963 shows no patch covering over the impact scar.

In 1997, Tague visited the U.S. National Archives and personally examined the curbstone scar chip. Tague was also accompanied by a U.S. National Archivist. They both immediately agreed that the scar chip was covered up with a foreign-material patch over the scar chip (no documented record nor documented authorization exists of precisely who or what agency had the scar chip within its evidence chain, nor when the scar chip was covered up). Harold Weisberg had said the same thing about the scar chip being covered over after he first examined the scar chip in the late 1960s.

In 2003, Tague wrote a book, *Truth Withheld* (ISBN 0-9718254-7-5), detailing his experiences during and after the assassination.

Source (edited): "http://en.wikipedia.org/wiki/James_Tague"

Jean Hill

Jean Hill (left), Mary Moorman (right) as captured in Frame 298 of the Zapruder film, just less than one second before the fatal head shot.

Norma Jean Lollis Hill (February 11, 1931, Oklahoma – November 7, 2000, Dallas, Texas) was a witness to the assassination of U.S. President John F. Kennedy in Dallas, Texas on November 22, 1963. She was known as the "Lady in Red" because of the long red rain coat she wore that day, as seen in the Zapruder Film. She was portrayed in the film *JFK* by Ellen McElduff.

She was present along with her friend Mary Moorman across from the grassy knoll, and was one of the very closest witnesses to President Kennedy when the shots were fired at him. Moorman can be seen taking pictures in the Zapruder film, which Hill claims were taken and bleached out.

At Zapruder frame 313, when President Kennedy was shot in the head, Jean Hill was only 21 feet (6.4 m) away, leftward, and slightly behind President Kennedy.

She testified to the Warren Commission that after the assassination she watched a man running from near the Texas School Book Depository towards the picket fence area. After watching this man, Hill crossed the street and ran with many other witnesses and authorities who first ran towards the grassy knoll after the shots ended.

Mrs. Jean L. Hill stated that after the firing stopped she saw a white man wearing a brown overcoat and a hat running west away from the Depository Building in the direction of the railroad tracks. She has since stated when she saw a photo of Jack Ruby after his killing of Lee Harvey Oswald she now believes he was the man she saw running. You can see in the Zapruder film that she was clearly looking into the direction of the Texas School Book Depository while the president is right in front of her which appears to support her story of looking at someone running just after the assassination. There are no other witnesses who claim to have seen a man running toward the railroad tracks. Examination of all the available films of the area following the shooting, reexamination of the interviews with individuals in the vicinity of the shooting, and the interviews with members of the Dallas police department and the Dallas Country sheriff's office failed to corroborate Mrs. Hill's recollection or to reveal the identity of the man described by Mrs. Hill. (Warren Commission Report, p. 640)

In Jean Hill's Warren Commission testimony she stated that a Secret Service agent told her on November 22, right after the attack, that another Secret Service agent, watching from the court house, saw a bullet strike, "at my feet" and kick up debris.

Hill was also one of several witnesses who have stated that at the end of the assassination she saw smoke lingering near the grassy knoll picket fence corner, although she made no mention of this when discussing the grassy knoll in her Warren Commission testimony (testimony that she has since stated was fabricated by the commission in her book "The Last Dissenting Witness").

During her commission testimony she stated that as the limousine came abreast of her she saw what she thought was a small white dog between President Kennedy and his wife. As is documented in films and photos captured at Love Field, Mrs. Kennedy was also given a small bouquet of white chrysanthemums that she held, and had laid upon the limousine seat during the motorcade.

Many of her claims have been officially disputed (though some researchers that doubt the Warren commission consider her a reliable witness). She claimed that Jack Ruby was in Dealey Plaza when witnesses placed him in the offices of The Dallas Morning News.

Perhaps her most explosive claim, made in her book and in the video "Beyond JFK" (and other places) was that she actually saw a shooter on the grassy knoll. However, that was not part of her original testimony. On the day of the assassination, she was interviewed by Jimmy Darnell of WBAP-TV and asked "Did you see the person who fired the . . .?" Hill replied "No, I didn't see any person fired the weapon, I only heard it."

Hill always thought of herself as a survivor after some of the other witnesses to the assassination died shortly thereafter under supposedly mysterious circumstances. She has even claimed that she received death threats and that her brakes were cut shortly after the assassination. She co-wrote a 1992 book entitled *The Last Dissenting Witness*. In a June, 2000 interview with Len Osanic, Hill discussed her plans to publish another book in the near future. Hill died in December of that year, and the second book was not published.

Source (edited): "http://en.wikipedia.org/wiki/Jean_Hill"

Jerry Haynes

Jerome Martin "Jerry" Haynes (born January 31, 1927) is an American actor from Dallas, Texas. He is most well known as Mr. Peppermint, a role he played for 30 years as the host of one of the longest-running local children's shows in television, the Dallas-based *Mr. Peppermint* (1961–1969), which was retitled *Peppermint Place* for its second run (1975–1996). He also has a long career in local and regional theater and has appeared in more than 50 films. A 1944 graduate of Dallas' Woodrow Wilson High School, he is the father of musician and lead singer Gibby Haynes of the group Butthole Surfers.

In 1990, Haynes was inducted into Woodrow's Hall of Fame.

Acting career

The "Mr. Peppermint" years

Haynes began his most famous role in 1961, playing a character who wore a red- and white-striped jacket and straw hat and carried a candy-striped magic cane. The original show ran for nine years as a live show, with Mr. Peppermint talking with a variety of puppet characters and including everything from cartoons to French lessons.

Early in the run of his show, an accident of fate made Haynes the first to report the Kennedy assassination on local news, together with his program director, Jay Watson. During lunch on the day of the shooting, the two men watched the Presidential motorcade pass on Main Street, and less than a minute later heard the deadly shots after the limousine turned onto Elm Street. The men quickly located and interviewed eyewitnesses, going on the air shortly later:

During these early years, the show began at 7:30 AM and ran for one hour, competing in its last half hour with the national CBS broadcast of *Captain Kangaroo* but usually winning its time slot. National trends shifted, however, and in 1970, the show was replaced by a talk program for the adult audience. After the Federal Communications Commission called in 1975 for more educational programming for children, the show was retooled as "Peppermint Place," a taped half-hour magazine-style program. The show continued in that format for over 20 years, eventually being syndicated to 108 markets nationwide before ending its run in 1996.

Other television and film work

Haynes in the 2007 Red River, New Mexico Fourth of July parade

Most of Haynes' film career has been in made-for-television films, especially those set in his native Texas. His first film role was in the 1981 docudrama *Crisis at Central High*, about the integration of Little Rock's Central High School, filmed in Dallas. Texas-themed films in which he has appeared — mostly based on true stories — include *Houston: The Legend of Texas* (1986), *A Killing in a Small Town* (1990, aka *Evidence of Love*), *Bonnie & Clyde: The True Story* (1992), *Texas Justice* (1995), *Don't Look Back* (1996), and *It's in the Water* (1997).

His chief feature film roles include 1984's *Places in the Heart*, as Deputy Jack Driscoll, and in the 1985 Patsy Cline biopic *Sweet Dreams* as Owen Bradley, Cline's record producer. He also played minor roles in *RoboCop* (1987) and *Boys Don't Cry* (1999).

He also has appeared as himself, partly through archive footage, in four documentary films discussing the Kennedy assassination: *Rush to Judgment* (1967), *11-22-63: The Day the Nation Cried* (1989), *Stalking the President: A History of American Assassins* (1992), and *Image of an Assassination: A New Look at the Zapruder Film* (1998).

In 1996 the Lone Star Film & Television Awards honored him with a Lifetime Achievement Award. He regularly appears in the Red River, New Mexico Fourth of July parade in a peppermint-colored Jeep.

Health

Haynes was diagnosed with Parkinson's disease in early 2008, and then was later diagnosed with a heart condition for which he received an artificial pacemaker. His doctors later revised their opinions to determine that he had a less aggressive form of Parkinson's.

Source (edited): "http://en.wikipedia.org/wiki/Jerry_Haynes"

John Connally

John Bowden Connally, Jr. (February 27, 1917 – June 15, 1993), was an influential American politician, serving as the 39th Governor of Texas, Secretary of the Navy under President John F. Kennedy, and as Secretary of the Treasury under President Richard M. Nixon. While he was Governor in 1963, Connally was a passenger in the car in which President Kennedy was assassinated. Connally was seriously wounded during the attack.

Early years, education, military

Connally was born into a large family in Floresville, the seat of Wilson County southeast of San Antonio. He was one of seven children born to Lela (née Wright) and John Bowden Connally, Sr., a dairy and tenant farmer. He was among the few Floresville High School graduates who attended college. Connally graduated from the University of Texas, where he was the student body president and a member of the Friar Society. He subsequently graduated from the University of Texas School of Law and was admitted to the bar by examination.

Connally served in the United States Navy during World War II, first as an aide to James V. Forrestal, then as part of the planning staff for the invasion of Africa by General Dwight D. Eisenhower. He transferred to the South Pacific Theater, where he served with distinction. He was a fighter-plane director aboard the aircraft carrier *USS Essex* and won a Bronze Star for bravery. He was shifted to another carrier, the *USS Bennington* and won a Legion of Merit. He was also involved in the campaigns in the Gilbert, Marshall, Ryukyu, and Philippine islands. He was discharged in 1946 at the rank of lieutenant commander.

On his release from the Navy, Connally practiced law but soon returned to Washington, D.C. to serve as a key aide to Lyndon Baines Johnson, when LBJ was a Congressman. He maintained close ties with Johnson until the former president's death in 1973.

Lawyer for Sid Richardson

Two of Connally's principal legal clients were the Texas oil tycoon Sid W. Richardson and Perry Bass, Richardson's nephew and partner, both of Fort Worth. Richardson's empire at the time was estimated at $200 million to $1 billion. Under Richardson's tutelage, Connally gained experience in a variety of enterprises and received tips on real estate purchases. The work required the Connallys to relocate to Fort Worth. When Richardson died in 1959, Connally was named to the lucrative position as co-executor of the estate.

Connally was also involved in a reported clandestine deal to place the Texas Democrat Robert Anderson on the 1956 Republican ticket as vice president. Though the idea fell through when Dwight Eisenhower retained Richard Nixon in the second slot, Anderson received a million dollars for his efforts and a subsequent appointment as treasury secretary, the same position that Connally would fill for Nixon fourteen years later in 1971. Moreover, in another irony, Anderson had been Eisenhower's first Navy secretary, the post that Connally filled for John F. Kennedy in 1961.

From Navy Secretary to Governor

At the 1960 Democratic convention in Los Angeles, Connally led supporters of Senator Lyndon Johnson. He claimed that John F. Kennedy, if nominated and elected, would be unable to serve as president for a full term because of Addison's disease and dependence on cortisone. Kennedy, however, had wrapped up the needed delegates for nomination before the convention even opened. Kennedy realized that he could not be elected without support of traditional Southern Democratic votes, many of whom had backed Johnson. Therefore, Johnson was offered the vice-presidential nomination.

Secretary of the Navy

At Johnson's request, in 1961 President Kennedy named Connally Secretary of the Navy. Connally resigned eleven months later to run for the Texas governorship. He had managed one of the largest employers in the world, as the Navy had more than 600,000 in uniform and 650,000 civilian workers, stationed at 222 bases in the United States and 53 abroad. It had a budget of $14 billion.

Connally directed the Sixth Fleet in the Mediterranean Sea on a new kind of "gunboat diplomacy". The USS Forrestal landed in Naples, Italy, and brought gifts to children in an orphanage. Connally ordered gifts also to a hospital in Cannes, France, which treated children with bone diseases; to poor Greek children on the island of Rhodes; and for spastic children in Palermo, Italy. Presents were also sent to Turkish children in Cyprus and to a camp in Beirut for homeless Palestinian refugees.

Connally fought hard to protect the Navy's role in the national space program, having vigorously opposed assigning most space research to the United States Air Force. *Time* magazine termed Connally's year as Navy secretary "a first-rate appointment". Critics noted, however, that the brevity of Connally's tenure precluded any sustained or comprehensive achievements.

Running for governor

Connally announced two weeks before Christmas of 1961 that he was leaving the position of navy secretary to return to Texas to seek the 1962 Democratic gubernatorial nomination. He would have to compete against the incumbent Marion Price Daniel, Sr., who was running for a fourth consecutive two-year term. Daniel was in political trouble following the enactment of a two-cent state sales tax in 1961, which had soured many voters on his administration. Daniel had let the tax become law without his signature but could have vetoed the measure. Former state Attorney General Will Wilson, who had run for the U.S. Senate vacated by Lyndon B. Johnson in 1961, also entered the gubernatorial campaign and was particularly critical of Johnson, whom he claimed engineered Connally's candidacy. Other primary candidates were highway commissioner Marshall Formby of Plainview, another party conservative, and General Edwin A. Walker, who made anti-communism the centerpiece of his campaign. Connally waged the most active campaign of any of the Democrats, having traveled more than 22,000 miles across the state. He made forty-three major speeches and appeared on multiple statewide and local telecasts.

Connally ran as a conservative Democrat. He was placed in a primary runoff election against the liberal attorney from Houston favored by organized labor, Don Yarborough, no relation to Connally's long-term party nemesis U. S. Senator Ralph W. Yarborough. After winning the runoff against Yarborough by a close vote, Connally faced a determined bid by the conservative Republican and oilfield equipment executive Jack Cox, also of Houston. Cox, a former state representative and a native of Stephens County, had run unsuccessfully two years earlier in the Democratic primary against Daniel. Connally received 847,036 ballots (54 percent) to Cox's 715,025 (45.6 percent). In the campaign, Connally made an issue of Cox's switching to the Republican Party (GOP) the previous year. Eleven years later, Connally made the same switch. Cox, as it turned out, was the strongest Republican gubernatorial candidate in Texas since 1924. Not until 1972, when Henry Grover carried the GOP banner, did the Republicans make a better showing for governor.

Connally was a master campaign professional. He believed in the entourage and advance men, the practice of having staff aides check out events in advance, and having press interviews on the run to demonstrate his heavy schedule of commitments. Biographer Charles Ashman claims that Connally would have aides telephone airports which he would shortly visit and ask to page him for an urgent message. Such manipulation, he believed, impressed airport patrons, many of whom would also be Texas voters.

Governor of Texas

Connally served as governor from 1963-1969. On November 22, 1963, Connally was seriously wounded while riding in President Kennedy's car in Dealey Plaza of Dallas when the president was assassinated. He recovered from wounds in his chest, wrist and thigh. The ten-month investigation by the Warren Commission of 1963–1964, the United States House Select Committee on Assassinations (HSCA) of 1977–1978, and other government investigations concluded that the President was assassinated by Lee Harvey Oswald. Connally did not dispute this conclusion, but did dispute the single bullet theory right up to the time of his death.

In the campaigns of 1964 and 1966, Connally defeated weak Republican challenges offered by Jack Crichton, a Dallas oil industrialist, and Thomas Everton Kennerly, Sr. (1903–2000), of Houston, respectively. He prevailed with margins of 73.8 percent and 72.8 percent, respectively, giving him greater influence with the nearly all-Democratic legislature.

In 1965, Connally appointed House Speaker Byron M. Tunnell to the Texas Railroad Commission, on the retirement of 32-year veteran Ernest O. Thompson, a former mayor of Amarillo. This appointment enabled Ben Barnes of De Leon in Comanche County to succeed Tunnell and become the youngest Speaker in Texas history.

After Charles Joseph Whitman, on August 1, 1966, went onto the University of Texas Tower in Austin and fired at people on the grounds and the surrounding community for over an hour and a half, Connally put together a Commission of experts who determined that Whitman had been suffering from a glioblastoma brain tumor, amphetamine abuse and had family troubles. All of the preceding issues contributed to the killing of sixteen on the campus and the wounding of many others, as well as the killing of his wife and mother in the early morning hours of August 1. Whitman himself was killed by ex-APD Officer Houston McCoy.

As governor, Connally promoted HemisFair '68, the world's fair held in San Antonio, he believed would net the state an additional $12 million in direct taxes. A permanent Institute of Texan Cultures museum was an outgrowth of the fair. It was designed to be "a dramatic showcase, not only to Texans, but to all the world, of the host of diverse peoples from many lands whose blood and dreams built our state."

During the Vietnam War, Connally hawkishly urged Johnson to "finish" the engagement by any military means necessary. Johnson, however, was more moderate in his conduct of the war than Connally advised.

There was some talk of Connally being picked as Hubert Humphrey's running mate in 1968, but the liberal Senator Edmund Muskie of Maine was chosen instead. Connally endorsed Humphrey and greeted the nominee at the Fort Worth airport and even reconciled for a month with intraparty rival Ralph Yarborough. Ashman claims that Connally was also "privately helping Nixon, recruiting a number of influential Texans, members of both parties, to work for the Republican candidate." Ben Barnes recounts a story that Connally in 1968 shouted at Humphrey in a private meeting at the Democratic National Convention in Chicago and accused the vice president of being disloyal to President Johnson by trying to soft-pedal Johnson's strong position regarding Vietnam. Barnes said that the "tongue-lashing" Connally gave Humphrey was "an epic. . . He orally spanked that man as hard as I've ever seen anyone chastised. He either strengthened Hubert's backbone, or gave him some, or scared him half to death."

Connally was succeeded as governor by Lieutenant Governor Preston Smith, a theater owner from Lubbock, who twice defeated the Republican attorney Paul Eggers in 1968 and 1970. Eggers, a friend and later associate of Republican Senator John G. Tower, served as general counsel in the Treasury Department from 1969–1970, before Connally joined the Nixon Cabinet.

Secretary of the Treasury

In 1971, Republican President Nixon appointed the then Democrat Connally as Treasury Secretary. Before agreeing to take the appointment, however, Connally told Nixon that the president must find a position in the administration for George H.W. Bush, the Republican who had been defeated in November 1970 in a hard-fought U.S. Senate race against Democrat Lloyd M. Bentsen. Connally told Nixon that his taking the treasury post would embarrass Bush, who had "labored in the vineyards" for Nixon's election as president, while Connally had supported Humphrey. Ben Barnes, then the lieutenant governor and originally a Connally ally, claims in his autobiography that Connally's insistence saved Bush's political career because the then former U.S. representative and twice-defeated Senate candidate relied on appointed offices to build a resume by which to seek the presidency in 1980 and again in 1988. Nixon hence named Bush as ambassador to the United Nations in order to secure Connally's services at treasury. Barnes also said that he doubted George W. Bush could have become president in 2001 had Bush's father not first been given the string of federal appointments during the 1970s to strengthen the family's political viability.

On taking the treasury post, Connally famously told a delegation of Europeans worried about exchange rate fluctuations that the American dollar "is our currency, but your problem."

Connally's official Treasury Department portrait

Secretary Connally defended a $50 billon increase in the debt ceiling and a $35 to $40 billion budget deficit as an essential "fiscal stimulus" at a time when five million Americans were unemployed. He unveiled Nixon's program of raising the price of gold and formally devaluing the dollar—finally leaving the old gold standard entirely, a process begun in 1934 by Franklin D. Roosevelt. Prices continued to increase during 1971, and Nixon allowed wage and price guidelines, which Congress had authorized on a stand-by basis, to be implemented. Connally later shied away from his role in recommending the failed wage and price controls. Connally announced guaranteed loans for the ailing Lockheed aircraft company. He fought a lonely battle too against growing balance-of-payment problems with the nation's trading partners. He also undertook important foreign diplomatic trips for Nixon through his role as Treasury Secretary.

Historian Bruce Schulman wrote that Nixon was "awed" by the handsome, urbane Texan who was also a tough political fighter. Schulman added that Henry Kissinger, Nixon's National Security Advisor, noted that Connally was the only cabinet member that Nixon did not disparage behind his back, and that this was high praise indeed.

Democrats for Nixon

Connally stepped down as treasury secretary in 1972 to head "Democrats for Nixon", a group funded by Republicans. Connally's old mentor, Lyndon Johnson, stood behind Democratic presidential nominee George S. McGovern of South Dakota, although McGovern had long opposed Johnson's foreign and defense policies. It was the first time that Connally and Johnson were on opposite sides of a general election campaign. Connally's brother, Golfrey Connally, an economics professor at a junior college in San Antonio, also endorsed McGovern. Some evidence even suggests that Connally was "privately" for Eisenhower in 1952 and 1956, instead of the Democratic candidate Adlai E. Stevenson of Illinois, for whom Johnson campaigned with considerable loyalty. During the war, Connally had served on Eisenhower's planning staff for the invasion of North Africa.

In the 1972 U.S. Senate election in Texas, Connally endorsed the Democratic Harold Barefoot Sanders, later a federal judge from Dallas, rather than the Republican incumbent John G. Tower, also of Dallas. Connally had considered running against Tower in 1966, but chose to run for a third term as governor. Tower then defeated a Connally ally, state Attorney General Waggoner Carr of Lubbock.

Tower, Nixon's choice in the Senate race, won handily over Sanders, but the Republican candidate for governor, Henry Grover of Houston, a victim of intraparty maneuvering, fell short and lost to Democrat Dolph Briscoe of Uvalde, a city in South Texas.

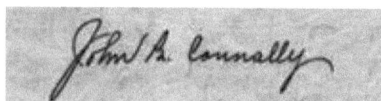

Connally's signature, as used on American currency

In January 1973, Lyndon Johnson died of heart disease. He and Connally had been friends since 1938. Connally took part in eulogizing Johnson during interment services at the LBJ Ranch in Gillespie County, along with the Rev. Billy Graham, who officiated at the service.

Switching parties

In May 1973, Connally joined the Republican Party. When Vice President Spiro Agnew resigned five months later because of scandal, Connally was one of Nixon's potential choices to fill the vacancy. Nixon tapped Gerald Rudolph Ford, Jr., the House Minority Leader from Grand Rapids, Michigan, because he believed that the moderate Ford could be easily confirmed by both houses of Congress, as required by the 25th Amendment to the United States Constitution. A Connally nomination presumably could have been blocked by liberal Democratic opposition. The weakened Nixon did not want a fight for the vice-presidential selection.

Connally's party bolt left a sour taste in the mouth of at least one prominent Texas Democrat who stood with George McGovern in 1972: Bob Bullock, the Hillsboro native who served as Texas secretary of state, comptroller and lieutenant governor: "...I got some ideas on Mr. Connally. He ain't never done nothin' but get shot in Dallas. He got the silver bullet. He needs to come back here and get hisself [sic] shot once every six months. I attack Connally on his vanity. He's terribly bad [sic] vain, y'know..."

In 1975, Connally was accused of pocketing $10,000 for influencing a milk price decision by Texas lawyer Jake Jacobsen. At his trial, he called as character witnesses Jackie Kennedy, Lady Bird Johnson, Barbara Jordan (the first African American woman state senator in Texas history), Dean Rusk, Robert McNamara, and Billy Graham. Connally was acquitted.

Running for President

Connally announced in January 1979 that he would seek the Republican nomination for President in 1980. He was considered a great orator and strong leader and was featured on the cover of *Time* with the heading "Hot on the Trail". His wheeler-dealer image remained a liability. Connally raised more money than any other candidate, but he was never able to overtake the popular conservative front runner Ronald Reagan of California. Connally spent his money nationally, while George H. W. Bush, like Connally from Houston, targeted his time and money in early states and won the Iowa caucus. The Houston political activist Clymer Wright rejected both Connally and Bush and served as Reagan's finance chairman in Texas. Bush's status as a challenger to Reagan was at first heightened by his victory in Iowa.

Connally focused on South Carolina, an early primary state in which he had the support of popular U.S. Senator Strom Thurmond, but he lost there to Reagan 55 to 30 percent and withdrew from the contest. After spending $11 million during the campaign, Connally secured the support of only a single delegate, Ada Mills of Clarksville, Arkansas, who became nationally known for a brief time as the "$11 million delegate".

Connally quickly endorsed Reagan, appeared with the former governor at the Dallas-Fort Worth Airport, and helped Reagan to win a narrow primary victory over Bush in Texas.

Connally said that he and Bush despised each other. The statement seemed to contradict Connally's earlier insistence that President Nixon name Bush to a post in the administration as a pre-condition for Connally's agreeing to become treasury secretary. Rumors also abounded in 1964 that Connally personally voted for Bush for senator because of his greater dislike for Bush's then opponent, Senator Ralph Yarborough. Charles Keating once contributed to Connally's campaign for President.

Later years

In 1986, Connally filed for bankruptcy as a result of a string of business losses in Houston. In December 1990, Connally and Oscar Wyatt, chairman of the Coastal Oil Corporation, met with President Saddam Hussein of Iraq. Hussein had been holding foreigners as hostages (or "guests" as Hussein called them) at strategic military sites in Iraq. After the meeting Hussein agreed to release the hostages.

Connally was known as an immaculate dresser who wore expensive and stylish suits wherever he went. Biographer Charles Ashman related a story about Connally's carrying a cigarette lighter in his pocket and lighting cigarettes as a courtesy only for very wealthy men who might be inclined to contribute to his political causes or retain him as a consultant on business arrangements.

The Connally Memorial Medical Center on U.S. Highway 181 in Floresville

In one of his last political acts, Connally endorsed then Republican U.S. Representative Jack Fields of Houston in the special election called in May 1993 to fill the vacancy left by U.S. Senator Lloyd Bentsen of Houston. Bentsen was appointed Treasury Secretary in the new administration of Bill Clinton. Fields finished fourth in the special election and left Congress thereafter. Republican Kay Bailey Hutchison, for whom Connally's daughter had been employed in the state treasurer's office, won the seat by a wide margin in the special election runoff against the appointed Democratic Senator Robert Krueger.

Death

Connally tombstone at Texas State Cemetery in Austin, Texas

Connally died of pulmonary fibrosis, a progressive scarring of the lungs. His funeral was held at the First United Methodist Church of Austin where he and his wife, Nellie Connally, had been members since their days living one block to the south in the Texas Governors Mansion, 1963-1969. The Connallys are interred at the Texas State Cemetery in Austin.

Former President Nixon left the bedside of his wife, Pat Nixon, who died a week later, and flew to Austin to attend Connally's funeral. The Connally Loop (Interstate Inner Loop 410) in San Antonio is named in his honor. The Connally Memorial Medical Center in Floresville is named for John, Wayne, and Merrill Connally. The John Connally Unit of the Texas Corrections Department south of Kenedy in Karnes County is named in his honor. There is also a Connally Plaza, with a life-sized statue of Connally, in downtown Houston.

Source (edited): "http://en.wikipedia.org/wiki/John_Connally"

Kenneth O'Donnell

Kenneth Patrick O'Donnell (March 4, 1924 – September 9, 1977), known as **Kenny**, was a top aide to U.S. President John F. Kennedy and part of the group of Kennedys' close advisors called the "Irish Mafia". He served as organizer and director of Kennedy's presidential campaign schedule in 1960, as Kennedy's special assistant and appointments secretary 1961–1963, as Lyndon Johnson's Presidential Aide 1963–1965, and as campaign manager for Robert Kennedy in the 1968 presidential election campaign and, after Kennedy's assassination, for Hubert Humphrey.

Early life and studies

Born **Patrick Kenneth O'Donnell** in Worcester, Massachusetts, O'Donnell's first and middle names were legally switched in the 1960s. His father, Cleo O'Donnell, was the football coach for the Holy Cross Crusaders football team for two decades and later athletics director for all sports activities at the College of the Holy Cross. O'Donnell had an older brother, Cleo, who was a football star at Harvard during the 1940s.

During World War II O'Donnell served in the US Army Air Corps (1942–1945). After completing his service in the AAC, he studied at Harvard College 1946–1949. It was at Harvard that O'Donnell met Robert Kennedy, where they were roommates as well as teammates on the Harvard football team; O'Donnell became team captain in 1948. O'Donnell and Robert Kennedy remained close friends until Kennedy's assassination in 1968.

While at Harvard, O'Donnell married his wife, Helen, in 1947. They had five children, among them entrepreneur Kevin M. O'Donnell – in 1950 – and writer Helen O'Donnell – in 1962. Following graduation from Harvard, O'Donnell attended law school at Boston College from 1950–51. He later worked as a salesman for the Hollingsworth Paper Company and then the Whitney Corporation, both in Boston, from 1951–52. O'Donnell later worked in public relations from 1952–57.

Political career

O'Donnell's friendship with Bobby Kennedy found him involved with the Kennedy family's political career already in 1946, when Bobby enlisted him to work for John F. Kennedy's first congressional campaign, and in 1952 the two campaigned together to get JFK elected to the United States Senate. O'Donnell then went on to serve as JFK's unpaid political observer in

Massachusetts, until he in 1957 was employed as assistant counsel of the 1957–59 Senate Labor Rackets Committee by Robert Kennedy, who had been appointed chief counsel of the committee.

In 1958, O'Donnell became a member of JFK's staff, and in 1960 he was the organizer and director of John F. Kennedy's presidential campaign schedule. The following year he became Kennedy's special assistant and Appointments Secretary. In this role he functioned in many ways as Kennedy's Chief of Staff, a position that Kennedy never filled during his tenure in the White House.

O'Donnell unofficially advised Kennedy during the planning for the Bay of Pigs invasion as well as during the 1962 Cuban missile crisis, and was an early critic of the Vietnam War, advising Kennedy to bring an end to America's involvement in the conflict.

O'Donnell arranged JFK's trip to Dallas in November 1963, and was in a car just behind the president's when Kennedy was assassinated. It was an enormous blow to O'Donnell, who long blamed himself for the death of the president.

After having served as a Presidential Aide to Lyndon Johnson until 1965, O'Donnell tried to win the Democratic nomination for the election for Massachusetts Governor in 1966, losing by only 64,000 votes to Edward McCormack, which was much less than the polls had predicted. In 1968, he served as campaign manager for Robert Kennedy, when Kennedy challenged President Johnson for renomination.

Following Robert Kennedy's assassination in Los Angeles on June 5, 1968, which was an even worse blow to O'Donnell than the assassination of JFK five years earlier, he joined, as did many others in Kennedy's campaign, Hubert Humphrey's presidential campaign, serving as campaign manager for Humphrey as well.

In 1970, he made another attempt to win the Democratic nomination for the election for Massachusetts Governor, but finished fourth in a primary field of four Democrats, with just 9 percent of the vote.

The combination of personal electoral disappointments and the assassinations of his two best friends drove him to increasing levels of alcoholism. He died in September 1977, just months after his wife Helen.

Praise

In his biography *With Kennedy* (1966), Pierre Salinger writes:

" It was my impression that O'Donnell had the greatest influence in shaping the President's most important decisions. He was able to set aside his own prejudices against individuals and his own ideological commitments (I would rate him a moderate Democrat) and appraise the alternatives with total objectivity. It was impossible to categorize O'Donnell, as White House observers did with other staff members, as either a "hawk" or a "dove" on foreign policy, or a Stevenson liberal or Truman conservative on civil rights. JFK gave extra weight to O'Donnell's opinions because he knew he had no personal cause to argue. Ken had only one criterion: Will this action help or hurt the President? And that, for " O'Donnell, was another way of asking: Will it help or hurt the country?

Criticism

In his autobiography *Counselor*, Ted Sorensen (who served as special counsel to President Kennedy) claims that O'Donnell polarized the JFK staff into the professional "politicians" and the academicians (such as Sorensen and Arthur Schlesinger). Sorensen also claims that O'Donnell's antipathy towards himself ran so deep that he in 1976/77 worked to derail Sorensen's nomination as Director of Central Intelligence for Jimmy Carter.

Writing

O'Donnell and David Powers co-authored *"Johnny We Hardly Knew Ye": Memories of John Fitzgerald Kennedy* (Boston: Little, Brown & Co., 1972). ISBN 0316716251

In 1998, his daughter, freelance writer Helen O'Donnell, wrote a biography about her father and his close friendship with Bobby Kennedy: *A Common Good: The Friendship of Robert F. Kennedy and Kenneth P. O'Donnell*.

Portrayal in media

- *The Missiles of October* (1974, TV): played by Stewart Moss
- *Kennedy* (1983, TV): played by Trey Wilson
- *JFK* (1991): played by David Benn
- *A Woman Named Jackie* (1991):played by Clark Gregg
- *Thirteen Days* (2000): played by Kevin Costner.
- *Jackie Bouvier Kennedy Onassis* (2000, TV): played by Brian Wrench

Source (edited): "http://en.wikipedia.org/wiki/Kenneth_O%27Donnell"

Lee Bowers

Lee Edward Bowers, Jr. (January 12, 1925, Dallas, Texas – August 9, 1966, Dallas, Texas) was a key witness to the assassination of John F. Kennedy in Dallas, Texas in 1963. At the moment of the assassination he was operating the Union Terminal Company's two-story interlocking tower, overlooking the parking lot just north of the grassy knoll and west of the Texas School Book Depository. He had an unobstructed view of the rear of the concrete pergola and the stockade fence atop the knoll. He described hearing three shots that came from either the Depository on his left or near the mouth of the Triple Underpass railroad bridge on his right; he was unsure because of the reverberation from the shots.

Bowers worked in the two-story railroad tower seen at the top of this photo of Dealey Plaza in Dallas, Texas

Warren Commission

When asked by the Warren Commission, "Now, were there any people standing on the high side — high ground between your tower and where Elm Street goes down under the underpass toward the mouth of the underpass?" Bowers testified that at the time the motorcade went by on Elm Street, four men were in the area: one or two uniformed parking lot attendants, one of whom Bowers knew; and two men standing 10 to 15 feet (3 to 5 m) apart near the Triple Underpass, who did not appear to know each other. One was "middle-aged, or slightly older, fairly heavy-set, in a white shirt, fairly dark trousers" and the other was "younger man, about midtwenties, in either a plaid shirt or plaid coat or jacket." One or both were still there when the first police officer arrived "immediately" after the shooting. Many assumed that Bowers meant that these men were standing behind the stockade fence at the top of the grassy knoll.

Rush to Judgment

However, two years later when Bowers was interviewed by assassination researchers Mark Lane and Emile de Antonio for their documentary film *Rush to Judgment*, he clarified that these two men were standing in the opening between the pergola and the stockade fence, and that "no one" was behind the fence when the shots were fired. Bowers said,

These two men were standing back from the street somewhat at the top of the incline and were very near two trees which were in the area. And one of them, from time to time as he walked back and forth, disappeared behind a wooden fence which is also slightly to the west of that. These two men to the best of my knowledge were standing there at the time of the shooting.

Photographs of the grassy knoll during the assassination show Dealey Plaza groundskeeper Emmett Hudson and a younger man, whom Hudson estimated was in his late twenties, standing on the stairway leading from Elm Street up to the stockade fence. Bowers was not sure if he could see the older man after the shootings, and a photograph shows Hudson sitting down on the steps at that time.

Employment

Bowers served in the U.S. Navy from ages 17 to 21. He attended Hardin-Simmons University for two years then Southern Methodist University for two years, majoring in religion. He worked for the Union Terminal Co. railyard for 15 years, also working as a self-employed builder. In 1964 he began working as business manager for a hospital and convalescent home.

Death

Bowers died in 1966 when his car left an empty road and struck a concrete abutment. It has often been claimed that his death was a murder, but investigator David Perry concludes that there is no basis for this belief.

Bowers was played by Pruitt Taylor Vince in the 1991 film *JFK*.

Source (edited): "http://en.wikipedia.org/wiki/Lee_Bowers"

Lee Harvey Oswald

Lee Harvey Oswald (October 18, 1939 – November 24, 1963) was, according to four government investigations, the sniper who killed John F. Kennedy, the 35th President of the United States, in Dallas, Texas, on November 22, 1963.

A former U.S. Marine who had briefly (October 1959 – June 1962) defected to the Soviet Union, Oswald was initially arrested for the shooting murder of police officer J. D. Tippit, on a Dallas street approximately 40 minutes after Kennedy was shot. Suspected in the assassination of Kennedy as well, Oswald denied involvement in either of the killings. Two days later, while being transferred from police headquarters to the county jail, Oswald was shot and killed by nightclub owner Jack Ruby in full view of television cameras broadcasting live.

In 1964, the Warren Commission concluded that Oswald acted alone in assassinating Kennedy, firing three shots, a conclusion also reached by prior investigations carried out by the FBI and Dallas Police Department. However, in 1979, the House Select Committee on Assassinations concluded that Oswald 'probably' did not act alone. The evidence used to base this conclusion has since been widely disputed.

Early life

Childhood

Oswald was born in New Orleans on October 18, 1939, to Robert Edward Lee Oswald, Sr. (New Orleans, Louisiana, March 4, 1896 – New Orleans, August 19, 1939) and Marguerite Frances Claverie (New Orleans, Louisiana, July 19, 1907 – Fort Worth, Texas, January 17, 1981). Oswald had two older siblings – brother Robert Edward Lee Oswald, Jr. and half-brother John Edward Pic.

Oswald's father died prior to Oswald's birth, and Marguerite raised her sons alone. When Oswald was two, his mother placed her sons at the Bethlehem Children's Home orphanage in New Orleans for thirteen months, as she was unable to support them. On May 7, 1945, his mother married Edwin Albert Ekdahl (1895–1953) in Fort Worth, Texas; he engaged in numerous extramarital affairs and filed for divorce in 1948.

As a child, Oswald was withdrawn and temperamental. In August 1952, while living with half-brother John Pic, at the time a U.S. Coast Guardsman stationed in New York City, Oswald and Marguerite were asked to leave after Oswald allegedly threatened Pic's wife with a knife and struck their mother, Marguerite.

Charges of truancy, in the Bronx (NYC), led to psychiatric assessment at a juvenile reformatory, the psychiatrist, Dr. Renatus Hartogs, describing Oswald's "vivid fantasy life, turning around the topics of omnipotence and power, through which he tries to compensate for his present shortcomings and frustrations." Finding a "personality pattern disturbance with schizoid features and passive-aggressive tendencies," Dr. Hartogs recommended continued treatment. However, in January 1954, Oswald's mother Marguerite returned with him to New Orleans. At the time, there was a question pending before a New York judge as to whether Oswald should be removed from the care of his mother to finish his schooling, although his behavior appeared to improve during his last months in New York.

In New Orleans, in October 1955, Oswald left the 10th grade after one month. He worked as an office clerk or messenger around New Orleans, rather than attend school. Planning for his enlistment, the family returned to Fort Worth in July 1956, and he re-enrolled in 10th grade for the September session, but quit in October to join the Marines (see below); he never received a high school diploma. By the of age 17, he had resided at 22 different locations and attended 12 different schools.

Though he had trouble spelling and writing coherently he read voraciously, and by age 15 claimed to be a Marxist, writing in his diary, "I was looking for a key to my environment, and then I discovered socialist literature. I had to dig for my books in the back dusty shelves of libraries." At 16 he wrote to the Socialist Party of America for information on their Young People's Socialist League, saying he had been studying socialist principles for "well over fifteen months." However, Edward Voebel, "whom the Warren Commission had established was Oswald's closest friend during his teenage years in New Orleans...said that reports that Oswald was already 'studying Communism' were a 'lot of baloney.' " Voebel said that "Oswald commonly read 'paperback trash.'"

Marine Corps

LEE HARVEY OSWALD AS A MARINE

COMMISSION EXHIBIT No. 2894

Oswald when he served in the US Marine Corps

Oswald enlisted in the United States Marine Corps on October 24, 1956, just after his seventeenth birthday. He idolized his older brother Robert and a photograph, after his arrest by Dallas police, shows Lee wearing his brother's Marines ring. One witness testified to the Warren Commission that Oswald's enlistment may also have been an escape from his overbearing mother.

Oswald's primary training was as a radar operator, a position requiring a security clearance. A May 1957 document states that he was "granted final clearance to handle classified matter up to and including CONFIDENTIAL after careful check of local records had disclosed no derogatory data." In the Aircraft Control and Warning Operator Course he finished seventh in a class of thirty. The course "...included instruction in aircraft surveillance and the use of radar." He was assigned first to Marine Corps Air Station El Toro in July 1957, then to Naval Air Facility Atsugi in Japan in September as part of Marine Air Control Squadron 1.

Like all Marines, Oswald was trained and tested in shooting, scoring 212 in December 1956 (slightly above the minimum for qualification as a *sharpshooter*) but in May 1959 scoring only 191 (barely earning the lower designation of *marksman*).

Oswald was court-martialed after accidentally shooting himself in the elbow with an unauthorized handgun, then court-martialed again for fighting with a sergeant he thought responsible for his punishment in the shooting matter. He was demoted from private first class to private and briefly imprisoned. He was later punished for a third incident: while on night-time sentry duty in the Philippines, he inexplicably fired his rifle into the jungle.

Slightly built, Oswald was nicknamed *Ozzie Rabbit* after the cartoon character, or sometimes *Oswaldskovich* because of his pro-Soviet sentiments. In December 1958 he transferred back to El Toro, where his unit's function "...was to serveil [sic] for aircraft, but basically to train both enlisted men and officers for later assignment overseas." An officer there termed Oswald a "very competent" crew chief.

While in the Marines, Oswald made an effort to teach himself rudimentary Russian. Although an unusual accomplishment, in February 1959 he was invited to take a Marine proficiency exam in written and spoken Russian. His effort at the time was rated "poor".

Adult life and early crimes

Defection to the Soviet Union

In October 1959, just before turning 20, Oswald traveled to the Soviet Union, the trip planned well in advance. On September 11, 1959, he received a hardship discharge from active service, claiming his mother needed care, and was put on reserve. Along with his self-taught Russian, he had saved $1,500 of his Marine Corps salary, obtained a passport, and submitted several fictional applications to foreign universities in order to obtain a student visa. Oswald spent two days with his mother in Fort Worth, then embarked by ship from New Orleans on September 20 to Le Havre, France, then immediately proceeded to England. Arriving in Southampton on October 9, he told officials he had $700 and planned to remain in the United Kingdom for one week before proceeding to a school in Switzerland. But on the same day, he flew to Helsinki, where he was issued a Soviet visa on October 14. Oswald left Helsinki by train on the following day, crossed the Soviet border at Vainikkala, and arrived in Moscow on October 16.

Almost immediately, Oswald told his Intourist guide of his desire to become a Soviet citizen, but was told on October 21 that his application had been refused. Oswald then inflicted a minor but bloody wound to his left wrist in his hotel room bathtub, after which the Soviets put him under psychiatric observation at a hospital.

On October 31, Oswald appeared at the United States embassy in Moscow, declaring a desire to renounce his U.S. citizenship. Oswald told the interviewing officer at the U.S. embassy, Richard Snyder, "...that he had been a radar operator in the Marine Corps and that he had voluntarily stated to unnamed Soviet officials that as a Soviet citizen he would make known to them such information concerning the Marine Corps and his specialty as he possessed. He intimated that he might know something of special interest." (Such statements led to Oswald's *hardship/honorable* military discharge being changed to *undesirable*.) The Associated Press story of the defection of a U.S. Marine to the Soviet Union was reported on the front pages of some newspapers in 1959.

Marina Prusakova, Minsk 1959

Though Oswald had wanted to attend Moscow University, he was sent to Minsk to work as a lathe operator at the Gorizont (Horizon) Electronics Factory, a facility producing radios, televisions, and military and space electronics. He also received a subsidized, fully furnished studio apartment in a prestigious building and an additional supplement to his factory pay—all in all, an idyllic existence by Soviet working-class standards, although he was under constant surveillance.

But Oswald grew bored in Minsk. He wrote in his diary in January 1961: "I am starting to reconsider my desire about staying. The work is drab, the money I get has nowhere to be spent. No nightclubs or bowling alleys, no places of recreation except the trade union dances. I have had enough." Shortly afterwards, Oswald (who had never formally renounced his U.S. citizenship) wrote to the U.S. Embassy in Moscow requesting return of his American passport, and proposing to return to the U.S. if any charges against him would be dropped.

In March 1961, Oswald met Marina Nikolayevna Prusakova, a 19-year-old pharmacology student; they married less than six weeks later in April. The Oswalds' first child, June, was born on February 15, 1962. On May 24, 1962, Oswald and Marina applied at the U.S. Embassy in Moscow for documents enabling her to immigrate to the U.S. and, on June 1, the U.S. Embassy gave Oswald a repatriation loan of $435.71. Oswald, Marina, and their infant daughter left for the United States, where they received no attention from the press, much to Oswald's disappointment.

Dallas

The Oswalds soon settled in the Dallas/Fort Worth area, where his mother and brother Robert lived, and Oswald began a memoir on Soviet life. Though he eventually gave up the project, his search for literary feedback put him in touch with anti-Communist Russian émigrés in the area. In testimony given before the Warren Commission, Alexander Kleinlerer said that the Russian émigrés sympathized with Marina, while merely tolerating Oswald who they regarded as rude and arrogant.

Although the Russian émigrés eventually abandoned Marina when she made no sign of leaving Oswald, Oswald found an unlikely friend in 51-year-old Russian émigré George de Mohrenschildt, a well-educated petroleum geologist with intelligence connections. (A native of Russia, de Mohrenschildt told the Warren Commission that Oswald had a "...remarkable fluency in Russian.") Marina, meanwhile, befriended Ruth Paine, a Quaker who was trying to learn Russian, and her husband Michael who worked for Bell Helicopter. (Ruth Paine said that she first met the Oswalds at a party arranged by George de Mohrenschildt.)

In July 1962, Oswald was hired by Dallas' Leslie Welding Company; he disliked the work and quit after three months. In October, he was hired by the graphic-arts firm of Jaggars-Chiles-Stovall as a photoprint trainee. (George de Mohrenschildt's wife and daughter said that it was George de Mohrenschildt who secured the job at Jaggars-Chiles-Stovall for Oswald.) Oswald's inefficiency and rudeness at his new job were such that fights threatened to break out, and he was seen reading a Russian publication, *Krokodil*. He was fired during the first week of April 1963. He may have used equipment at the firm to forge identification documents.

Attempt on life of General Walker

Marina Oswald testified to the Warren Commission that Lee Harvey Oswald confessed to her on the night of April 10, 1963, that he shot at General Edwin Walker with his rifle, and buried the rifle that night. The Warren Commission concluded that on April 10, 1963, Oswald attempted to kill retired U.S. Major General Edwin Walker, an outspoken anti-communist, segregationist, and member of the John Birch Society. In 1961, Walker had been relieved of his command of the 24th Division of the U.S. Army in West Germany for distributing right-wing literature to his troops. Walker's later actions in opposition to racial integration at the University of Mississippi led to his arrest on insurrection, seditious conspiracy, and other charges. He was temporarily held in a mental institution on orders from President Kennedy's brother, Attorney General Robert Kennedy, but a grand jury refused to indict him. Oswald's wife, Marina told the Warren Commission that Oswald considered Walker the leader of a "fascist organization."

In March 1963, Oswald purchased a 6.5 mm caliber Carcano rifle (commonly but improperly called Mannlicher-Carcano) by mail-order, using the alias *A. Hidell*, as well as a .38 Smith & Wesson Model 10 revolver by the same method.

The Warren Commission concluded that Oswald fired at Walker through a window, from less than 100 feet (30 m) away, as Walker sat at a desk in his home; the bullet struck the window-frame and Walker's only injury was bullet fragments to the forearm. Marina testified to the Warren Commission that Oswald told her that he had shot at Walker. (The United States House Select Committee on Assassinations stated that the "evidence strongly suggested" that Oswald carried out the shooting.)

Before the Kennedy assassination, Dallas police had no suspects in the Walker shooting, but Oswald's involvement was suspected within hours of his arrest following the assassination. (A note Oswald left for Marina on the night of the attempt, telling her what to do if he did not return, was not found until early December 1963.) The Walker bullet was too damaged to run conclusive ballistics studies on it, but neutron activation analysis later showed that it was "extremely likely" that it was made by the same manufacturer and for the same rifle make as the two bullets which later struck Kennedy.

George De Mohrenschildt, friend of the Oswalds when they were in Dallas, told the Warren Commission that he strongly suspected that Oswald took a 'pot shot' at General Walker, because the following weekend, on the night of Easter Sunday, April 14, 1963, George and Jeanne De Morhenschildt brought an Easter bunny to baby June Oswald, and when Marina was showing Jeanne their new apartment, Oswald's dug-up rifle appeared in a closet. Jeanne exclaimed to George that Lee had a rifle, and George joked to Lee, "Were you the one who took a pot-shot at General Walker?" At this point Lee and Marina both became stunned for an uncomfortable moment of silence, and then George broke the ice by laughing, and they all laughed. George De Mohrenschildt testified that this was the last time he ever saw Oswald, and that he had a strong feeling that Oswald was guilty of the shooting at General Walker.

New Orleans

Oswald passing out "Fair Play for Cuba" leaflets in New Orleans, August 16, 1963

Oswald rented an apartment in this building in Uptown New Orleans c. May–September 1963

Oswald's mugshot following his arrest in New Orleans

Oswald returned to New Orleans on April 24, 1963. Marina's friend, Ruth Paine, drove her by car from Dallas to join Oswald in New Orleans the next month in May. On May 10, Oswald was hired by the Reily Coffee Company whose owner (William Reily) was a backer of the Crusade to Free Cuba Committee, an anti-Castro organization. Oswald worked as a machinery greaser at Reily, but he was fired in July "...because his work was not satisfactory and because he spent too much time loitering in Adrian Alba's garage next door, where he read rifle and hunting magazines."

On May 26, Oswald wrote to the New York City headquarters of the pro-Castro Fair Play for Cuba Committee, proposing to rent "...a small office at my own expense for the purpose of forming a FPCC branch here in New Orleans." Three days later, the FPCC responded to Oswald's letter advising against opening a New Orleans office "at least not ... at the very beginning." In a follow-up letter, Oswald replied, "Against your advice, I have decided to take an office from the very beginning."

Then New Orleans District Attorney Jim Garrison noted in his book, "On the Trail of the Assassins", that officers of the FPCC, were allowed easy entry into Cuba. Oswald's rush to be considered a leading officer of the FPCC, without the permission of FPCC leaders, was considered suspicious by the FPCC, according to FPCC Tampa chapter President, Vincent T. Lee, in his testimony to the Warren Commission within volume 10 of the Warren Report.

As the sole member of the New Orleans chapter of the Fair Play for Cuba Committee, Oswald ordered the following items from a local printer: 500 application forms, 300 membership cards, and 1,000 leaflets with the heading, "Hands Off Cuba." According to Lee Oswald's wife Marina, Lee told her to sign the name "A.J. Hidell" as chapter president on his membership card.

On August 5 and 6, according to anti-Castro militant Carlos Bringuier, Oswald visited him at a store he owned in New Orleans. Bringuier was the New Orleans delegate for the Student Revolutionary Directorate (DRE), an anti-Castro organization. Bringuier would later tell the Warren Commission that he believed Oswald's visits were an attempt by Oswald to infiltrate his group. On August 9, Oswald turned up in downtown New Orleans handing out pro-Castro leaflets. Bringuier confronted Oswald, claiming he was tipped off about Oswald's leafleting by a friend. A scuffle ensued and Oswald, Bringuier, and two of Bringuier's friends were arrested for disturbing the peace. Before leaving the police station, Oswald asked to speak with an FBI agent. Agent John Quigley arrived and spent over an hour talking to Oswald. Nevertheless, both Oswald and Carlos Bringuier shared the same business address on 544 Camp Street in New Orleans.

A week later, on August 16, Oswald again passed out Fair Play for Cuba leaflets with two hired helpers, this time in front of the International Trade Mart. The incident was filmed by WDSU – the local TV station. The next day, Oswald was interviewed by WDSU radio commentator William Stuckey, who probed Oswald's background. A few days later, Oswald accepted Stuckey's invitation to take part in a radio debate with Carlos Bringuier and Bringuier's associate Edward Butler, head of the right-wing Information Council of the Americas (INCA).

One of Oswald's Fair Play for Cuba leaflets had the address "544 Camp Street" hand-stamped on it, apparently by Oswald himself. The address was in the "Newman Building" which, from October 1961 to February 1962, housed the militant anti-Castro group, the Cuban Revolutionary Council. Around the corner but located in the same building, with a different entrance, was the address 531 Lafayette Street—the address of "Guy Banister Associates", a private detective agency run by former FBI agent Guy Banister. Banister's office was involved in anti-Castro and intelligence activities in the New Orleans area.

In the late-1970s, the House Select Committee on Assassinations (HSCA) investigated the possible relationship of Oswald to Banister's office. While the committee was unable to interview Guy Banister (who died in 1964), the committee did interview his brother Ross Banister. Ross "...told the committee that his brother had mentioned seeing Oswald hand out Fair Play for Cuba literature on one occasion. Ross theorized that Oswald had used the 544 Camp Street address on his literature to embarrass Guy." However Jim Garrison notes that Oswald was photographed on the premises of 544 Camp Street, and that its main resident, Guy Banister, had been attempting to infiltrate the FPCC for years.

Guy Banister's secretary, Delphine Roberts, told author Anthony Summers that she saw Oswald at Banister's office, and that he filled out one of Banister's "agent" application forms. She said, "Oswald came back a number of times. He seemed to be on familiar terms with Banister and with the office." The House Select Committee on Assassinations investigated Roberts' claims and said that "because of contradictions in Roberts' statements to the committee and lack of independent corroboration of many of her statements, the reliability of her statements could not be determined."

Oswald's mid-1963 New Orleans activities were later investigated by New Orleans District Attorney Jim Garrison, as part of his prosecution of Clay Shaw in 1969. Garrison was particularly interested in an associate of Guy Banister—a man named David Ferrie and his possible connection to Oswald, which Ferrie himself denied. Ferrie died before Garrison could complete his investigation. Charged with conspiracy in the JFK assassination, Shaw was found not guilty.

In 1993, the PBS television program *Frontline* obtained a photograph, taken eight years before the assassination, showing Oswald and Ferrie at a Civil Air Patrol cookout with other C.A.P. cadets.

Mexico

Marina's friend, Ruth Paine, transported Marina and her child by car from New Orleans to the Paine home in Irving, Texas, near Dallas, on September 23, 1963. Oswald stayed in New Orleans at least two more days to collect a $33 unemployment check. It is uncertain when he left New Orleans: he is next known to have boarded a bus in Houston—bound for the Mexican border, rather than Dallas, and telling other passengers he planned to travel to Cuba via Mexico. In Mexico City, he applied for a transit visa at the Cuban Embassy, claiming he wanted to visit Cuba on his way back to the Soviet Union. Cuban officials insisted Oswald would need Soviet approval, but he was unable to get prompt co-operation from that embassy.

After five days of shuttling between consulates, a heated argument with the Cuban consul, impassioned pleas to

KGB agents, and at least some CIA scrutiny, Oswald was told by the Cuban consul that he was disinclined to approve the visa, saying "a person like [Oswald] in place of aiding the Cuban Revolution, was doing it harm." Nonetheless, on October 18, the Cuban embassy indeed approved the visa, but Oswald did not in fact embark for Cuba. (Eleven days before the assassination of Kennedy, Oswald wrote to the Soviet embassy in Washington, D.C., saying, "Had I been able to reach the Soviet Embassy in Havana as planned, the embassy there would have had time to complete our business.")

Return to Dallas

Texas Schoolbook Depository, where Oswald was an employee

Instead, on October 3, 1963, Oswald left by bus for Dallas. According to the Warren Commission, on October 14, a neighbor told Ruth Paine that there was a job opening at the Texas School Book Depository, an opening reported by her son Wesley Buell Frazier, who had a job there. Mrs. Paine informed Oswald, who was interviewed at the Depository and was hired there on October 16. Oswald's supervisor Roy Truly, said that Oswald "did a good day's work" and was an above average employee. During the week, Oswald stayed in a Dallas rooming house (under the name *O.H. Lee*), but he spent his weekends with Marina at the Paine home in Irving. Oswald did not drive, but commuted to and from Dallas on Mondays and Fridays with Wesley Frazier. On October 20, the Oswalds' second daughter was born. FBI agents twice visited the Paine home in early November, when Oswald was not present, looking for information on Marina, whom they suspected of being a Soviet agent. Oswald visited the Dallas FBI office about 7 to 10 days before the assassination, asking to see Special Agent James Hosty; told Hosty was unavailable, Oswald left a note that, according to the receptionist, read: "Let this be a warning. I will blow up the FBI and the Dallas Police Department if you don't stop bothering my wife. Signed—Lee Harvey Oswald." The note contained some sort of threat, but accounts varied widely as to whether Oswald threatened to "blow up the FBI" or merely "report this to higher authorities" Hosty testified to the Warren Commission that the note said, "If you have anything you want to learn about me, come talk to me directly. If you don't cease bothering my wife, I will take the appropriate action and report this to the proper authorities." According to Hosty, two days after the assassination, Dallas FBI Special Agent-in-Charge J. Gordon Shanklin ordered Hosty to destroy Oswald's note.

In the days before Kennedy's arrival, several newspapers described the route of the presidential motorcade as passing the Book Depository. On November 21 (a Thursday) Oswald asked Frazier for an unusual mid-week lift back to Irving, saying he had to pick up some curtain rods. The next morning (Friday) he returned to Dallas with Frazier; he left behind $170 and his wedding ring, but took with him a long paper bag. Oswald's co-worker, Charles Givens, testified that he saw Oswald on the sixth floor of the Depository at 11:55 a.m.—35 minutes before the assassination. However, another co-worker, Bonnie Ray Williams testified that he went to the sixth floor of the Depository to eat his lunch at about 12:05 p.m. and was there until at least 12:10 p.m. He said that during that time he did not see Oswald, or anyone else, on the sixth floor.

Shootings of Kennedy and Tippit

According to government investigations (including that of the Warren Commission) as Kennedy's motorcade passed through Dallas's Dealey Plaza about 12:30 p.m. on November 22, Oswald fired three rifle shots from the sixth-floor, southeast corner window of the Book Depository, killing the President and seriously wounding Texas Governor John Connally. Bystander James Tague received a minor facial injury.

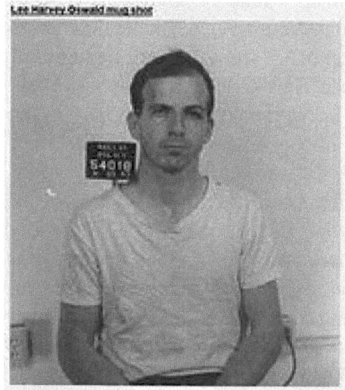

Dallas PD color mugshot November 23, 1963

According to the Warren Commission, immediately after firing, Oswald hid the rifle behind some boxes and descended using the rear stairwell. About ninety seconds after the shooting, in the second-floor lunchroom, he encountered police officer Marrion Baker accompanied by Oswald's supervisor Roy Truly; Baker let Oswald pass after Truly identified him as an employee. According to Baker, Oswald did not appear to be nervous or out of breath. (Baker initially wrote in his statement to the FBI that he "saw a man [who he would later identify as Oswald] standing in the lunchroom drinking a Coke." He subsequently crossed out the words "drinking a Coke" and there is no reference to the Coke in his Warren Commission testimony.) Mrs. Robert Reid, clerical supervisor at the Depository, returning to her office within two minutes of the assassination, said she saw Oswald who "was very calm" on the second-floor with a Coke in his hands. Oswald descended using the front staircase, and left the Depository through the front entrance just before police sealed it off. Oswald's supervisor, Roy Truly, later pointed out to officers that Oswald was the only employee to have left the building after the assassination.

At about 12:40 p.m., Oswald boarded a city bus but (probably due to heavy traffic) he requested a transfer from the driver and got off two blocks later. He took a taxicab to his rooming house, at 1026 North Beckley, arriving at about 1:00 p.m. He entered through the front door and, according to his housekeeper Earlene Roberts, immediately went to his room, "walking pretty fast". Mrs. Roberts testified that while Oswald was in his room, she witnessed a Dallas police car slowly pull up in front of the house, sound its horn twice, and then move slowly away. Mrs. Roberts testified that Oswald left "a very few minutes" later, zipping up a jacket he was not wearing when he had entered earlier, and that she last saw Oswald standing at a bus stop in front of the house.

Oswald was next witnessed near the corner of East 10th Street and North Patton Avenue, about nine-tenths of a mile (1.4 km) southeast of his rooming house—a distance that the Warren Commission said, "Oswald could have easily walked". According to the Warren Commission, it was here that Patrolman J. D. Tippit pulled alongside Oswald and "apparently exchanged words with [him] through the right front or vent window." At approximately 1:11–1:14 p.m., Tippit exited his car and was immediately struck and killed by four shots. Numerous witnesses heard the shots and saw a man flee the scene holding a revolver. Four cartridge cases found at the scene were identified by expert witnesses before the Warren Commission and the House Select Committee as having been fired from the revolver later found in Oswald's possession, to the exclusion of all other weapons.

Oswald's seat in the Texas Theater

Oswald being led from the Texas Theater after his arrest inside

Capture

Shoe store manager Johnny Brewer testified that minutes later he saw Oswald "ducking into" the entrance alcove of his store. Suspicious of this activity, Brewer watched Oswald continue up the street and slip into the nearby Texas Theater without paying. He alerted the theater's ticket clerk, who telephoned police at about 1:40 pm.

As police arrived, the house lights were brought up and Brewer pointed out Oswald sitting near the rear of the theater. Oswald appeared to surrender (saying, "Well, it is all over now") then struck an officer; he was disarmed after a struggle. As he was led from the theater, Oswald shouted he was a victim of police brutality.

At about 2 p.m., Oswald arrived at the Police Department building, where he was questioned by Detective Jim Leavelle about the shooting of Officer Tippit. When Captain J. W. Fritz heard Oswald's name, he recognized it as that of the Book Depository employee who was reported missing and was already a suspect in the assassination. Oswald was booked for both murders, and by the end of the night he had been arraigned as well.

Soon after his capture Oswald encountered reporters in a hallway, declaring "I didn't shoot anyone" and "They're taking me in because of the fact I lived in the Soviet Union. I'm just a patsy!" Later, at an arranged press meeting, a reporter asked, "Did you kill the President?" and Oswald, who by that time had been advised of the charge of murdering Tippit, but not yet arraigned in Kennedy's death, answered "No, I have not been charged with that. In fact, nobody has said that to me yet. The first thing I heard about it was when the newspaper reporters in the hall asked me that question." As he was led from the room, "What did you do in the USSR?" was called out, and "How did you hurt your eye?"; Oswald answered, "A policeman hit me."

Police interrogation

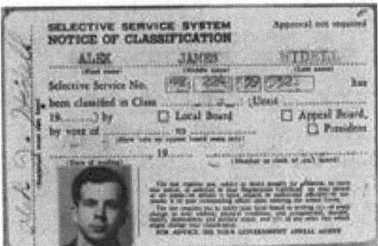
Fake selective service (draft) card in the name of *Alek James Hidell*, found on Oswald when arrested. *A.Hidell* was the name used on both envelope and order slip to buy the alleged murder weapon (see CE 773), and *A. J. Hidell* was the alternate name on the New Orleans post office box rented June 11, 1963, by Oswald. Both the alleged murder weapon and the pistol in Oswald's possession at arrest had earlier been shipped (at separate times) to Oswald's Dallas P.O. Box 2915, as ordered by "A. J. Hidell".

Oswald, handcuffed to Detective James Leavelle (light clothing), is shot by Jack Ruby.

The grave of Lee Harvey Oswald

Oswald was interrogated several times during his two days at Dallas Police Headquarters. He denied killing Kennedy and Tippit, denied owning a rifle, said two photographs of him holding a rifle and a pistol were fakes, denied telling his co-worker he wanted a ride to Irving to get curtain rods for his apartment, and denied carrying a long heavy package to work the morning of the assassination. The Warren Commission also noted that Oswald denied knowing an *A. J. Hidell,* and when shown a forged Selective Service card bearing that name in his possession when arrested, refused to answer any questions concerning it, saying "...you have the card yourself and you know as much about it as I do." The Warren Commission noted that this "spurious" card bore the name of *Alek James Hidell.*

During his first interrogation on Friday, November 22, Oswald was asked to account for himself at the time the President was shot. Oswald said he ate lunch in the Depository's first-floor lunchroom, then went to the second floor for a Coca-Cola, where he encountered a policeman. During his last interrogation on November 24, Oswald was asked again where he was at the time of the shooting; he said he was working on an upper floor when it occurred, then went downstairs where he encountered a policeman.

Oswald asked for legal representation several times while being interrogated, as well as in encounters with reporters. But when representatives of the Dallas Bar Association met with him in his cell on Saturday, he declined their services, saying he wanted to be represented by John Abt, chief counsel to the Communist Party USA, or by lawyers associated with the American Civil Liberties Union. Both Oswald and Ruth Paine tried to reach Abt by telephone several times Saturday and Sunday, but Abt was away for the weekend. Oswald also declined his brother Robert's offer on Saturday to obtain a local attorney.

Death

On Sunday, November 24, Oswald was being led through the basement of Dallas Police Headquarters preparatory to his transfer to the county jail when, at 11:21 a.m., Dallas nightclub operator Jack Ruby stepped from the crowd and shot Oswald in the abdomen. Oswald died at 1:07 p.m. at Parkland Memorial Hospital—the same hospital where Kennedy had died two days earlier.

A network television camera, there to cover the transfer, was broadcasting live at the time, and millions thereby witnessed the shooting as it happened. The event was also captured in a well-known photograph *(see right).* Ruby later said he had been distraught over Kennedy's death and that his motive for killing Oswald was "...saving Mrs. Kennedy the discomfiture of coming back to trial." Others have hypothesized that Ruby was part of a conspiracy.

After autopsy, Oswald was buried in Fort Worth's Rose Hill Memorial Burial Park. A marker inscribed simply *Oswald* replaces the stolen original tombstone, which gave Oswald's full name and birth–death dates.

Official investigations

Warren Commission

The Warren Commission, created by President Lyndon B. Johnson to investigate the assassination, concluded that Oswald acted alone in assassinating Kennedy (this view is known as the lone gunman theory). The Commission could not ascribe any one motive or group of motives to Oswald's actions: It is apparent, however, that Oswald was moved by an overriding hostility to his environment. He does not appear to have been able to establish meaningful relationships with other people. He was perpetually discontented with the world around him. Long before the assassination he expressed his hatred for American society and acted in protest against it. Oswald's search for what he conceived to be the perfect society was doomed from the start. He sought for himself a place in history — a role as the "great man" who would be recognized as having been in advance of his times. His commitment to Marxism and communism appears to have been another important factor in his motivation. He also had demonstrated a capacity to act decisively and without regard to the consequences when such action would further his aims of the moment. Out of these and the many other factors which may have molded the character of Lee Harvey Oswald there emerged a man capable of assassinating President Kennedy.

The proceedings of the commission were closed, though not secret, and about 3% of its files have yet to be released to the public, which has continued to provoke speculation among researchers.

Ramsey Clark Panel

In 1968, the Ramsey Clark Panel examined various photographs, X-ray films, documents, and other evidence, concluding that Kennedy was struck by two bullets fired from above and behind him, one of which traversed the base of the neck on the right side without striking bone, and the other of which entered the skull from behind and destroyed its right side.

House Select Committee

In 1979, after a review of the evidence and of prior investigations, the United States House Select Committee on Assassinations was preparing to issue a finding that Oswald had acted alone in killing Kennedy. However, late in the Committee's proceedings a Dictabelt was introduced, purportedly recording sounds heard in Dealey Plaza before, during and after the shots were fired. After submitting the Dictabelt to acoustic analysis, the Committee revised its findings to assert a "high probability that two gunmen fired" at

Kennedy and that Kennedy "was probably assassinated as the result of a conspiracy." Although the Committee was "unable to identify the other gunman or the extent of the conspiracy," it made a number of further findings regarding the likelihood or unlikelihood that particular groups, named in the findings, were involved.

The Dictabelt evidence has been questioned, some believing it is not a recording of the assassination at all. The staff director and chief counsel for the Committee, G. Robert Blakey, told ABC News in 2003 that at least 20 persons heard a shot from the grassy knoll, and that a conspiracy was established by both the witness testimony and acoustic evidence, but in 2004 he expressed less confidence. Officer H.B. McLain, from whose motorcycle radio the HSCA acoustic experts said the Dictabelt evidence came, has repeatedly stated that he was not yet in Dealey Plaza at the time of the assassination. McLain asked the Committee, "'If it was my radio on my motorcycle, why did it not record the revving up at high speed plus my siren when we immediately took off for Parkland Hospital?'"

In 1982, a group of twelve scientists appointed by the National Academy of Sciences (NAS), led by Norman Ramsey, concluded that the acoustic evidence submitted to the HSCA was "seriously flawed." Subsequently, a 2001 article in *Science and Justice*, the journal of Britain's Forensic Science Society, said that the NAS investigation was itself flawed and concluded with a 96.3 percent certainty that there were at least two gunmen firing at President Kennedy and that at least one shot came from the grassy knoll. Commenting on the British study, G. Robert Blakey said: "This is an honest, careful scientific examination of everything we did, with all the appropriate statistical checks."

Other investigations and dissenting theories

Image CE-133A, one of three known "backyard photos," the same image sent by Oswald (as a first-generation copy) to George de Mohrenschildt in April, 1963, dated and signed on the back. Oswald holds a Carcano rifle, with markings matching those on the rifle found in the Book Depository after the assassination.

Critics have not accepted the conclusions of the Warren Commission and have proposed a number of other theories, such as that Oswald conspired with others, or was not involved at all and was framed.

In October 1981, with Marina's support, Oswald's grave was opened to test a theory propounded by writer Michael Eddowes: that during Oswald's stay in the Soviet Union he was replaced with a Soviet double; that it was this double, not Oswald, who killed Kennedy and who is buried in Oswald's grave; and that the exhumed remains would therefore not exhibit a surgical scar Oswald was known to carry. However, dental records positively identified the exhumed corpse as Oswald's, and the scar was present.

Fictional trials

Several films have fictionalized a trial of Oswald. In 1988, a 21-hour unscripted mock trial was "held" on television, argued by actual lawyers before an actual judge, with unscripted testimony from surviving witnesses to the events surrounding the assassination; the mock jury returned a verdict of guilty.

Backyard photos

Lee Harvey Oswald's Carcano rifle, in the US National Archives

The "backyard photos", taken by Marina Oswald probably around March 31, 1963 using a camera belonging to Oswald, show Oswald holding two Marxist newspapers—*The Militant* and *The Worker*—and a rifle, and wearing a pistol in a holster. Shown the pictures after his arrest, Oswald insisted they were forgeries, but Marina testified in 1964 that she had taken the photographs at Oswald's request— testimony she reaffirmed repeatedly over the decades. These photos were labelled CE 133-A and CE 133-B. CE 133-A shows the rifle in Oswald's left hand and newsletters in front of his chest in the other, while the rifle is held with the right hand in CE 133-B. Oswald's mother testified that on the day after the assassination she and Marina destroyed another photograph with Oswald holding the rifle with both hands over his head, with "To my daughter June" written on it.

The HSCA obtained another first generation print (from CE 133-A) on April 1, 1977 from the widow of George de Mohrenschildt. The words "Hunter of fascists — ha ha ha!" written in block Russian were on the back. Also in English were added in script: "To my friend George, Lee Oswald, 5/IV/63 [April 5, 1963]" Handwriting experts for the HSCA concluded the English inscription and signature were by Oswald. After two original photos, one negative and one first-generation copy had been found, the Senate Intelligence Committee located (in 1976) a third backyard photo (CE 133-C) showing Oswald with newspapers held away from his body in his right hand). A test photo by the Dallas Police of a stand-in in the identical pose was released with the Warren Commission evidence in 1964, but it is not known why CE 133-C itself was not publicly acknowledged until a print was found in 1975 amongst the effects of a deceased Dallas police officer.

These photos, widely recognized as some of the most significant evidence against Oswald, have been subjected to rigorous analysis. Photographic experts consulted by the HSCA concluded they were genuine, answering twenty-one points raised by critics. Marina Oswald has always maintained she took the photos herself, and the 1963 de Mohrenschildt print bearing Oswald's signature clearly indicate they existed before the assassination. Nonetheless, some continue to contest their authenticity. After digitally analyzing the photograph of Oswald holding the rifle and paper, computer scientist Hany Farid concluded that the photo "almost certainly was not altered."

Source (edited): "http://en.wikipedia.org/wiki/Lee_Harvey_Oswald"

Linda Willis

Linda Kay Willis (born 1949) was a close witness during the assassination of President Kennedy.

Seen in the Zapruder film at the start of the assassination wearing a blue coat and a long gold skirt, located to the left of President Kennedy's limousine, on the south side of Elm Street, directly in front of the Texas School Book Depository.

Willis testified to the Warren Commission in 1964 that she remembered hearing three shots, with the last two shots bunched much closer together than the first two shots. Specifically, Willis testified that the assassination started when President Kennedy was already waving (his waving motion does not start until Zapruder film frame 174) when she heard the first shot that she remembered hearing (from Z-165 through Z-208 the president was hidden by a large oak tree from the view of anyone located in the Warren Commission lone snipers lair). Like many Dealey Plaza witnesses, the first shot she remembered hearing sounded to her like a firecracker. She testified that this first shot hit President Kennedy because she saw the president immediately and nearly simultaneously quickly raise both his arms and grab towards his throat as a result of the first shot she remembered. Willis testified that she did not know where the second shot that she remembered hearing came from or went to. Willis testified that it was the third shot that she remembered that hit President Kennedy in his head. In 1978 Willis testified to the House Select Committee on Assassinations that she "had a distinct impression that the head wound to President Kennedy was a result of a front-to-rear shot" when she saw his head "blow up." In her 1989 video interview for The Men Who Killed Kennedy documentary, Willis stated that when she saw the president's head explode in blood that she saw head matter came out the back of the president's head, so, the head shot must have been fired from the front of President Kennedy.

Willis stated to assassination researcher and author Richard Trask ("Pictures of the Pain" 1994) that after the assassination she and her sister Rosemary also saw someone find a piece of the president's head that had landed in the grass located at least twenty-two feet to the left of the president.

After the assassination Willis, along with her sister, father (Phillip), and mother (Marilyn) were present at the Kodak photographic laboratory getting her father's assassination related photo slides developed when the Zapruder film was first developed and first shown.

Source (edited): "http://en.wikipedia.org/wiki/Linda_Willis"

Marie Muchmore

Marie M. Muchmore (August 5, 1909, Ardmore, Oklahoma – April 26, 1990, Dallas, Texas) was one of the witnesses to the assassination of U.S. President John F. Kennedy in Dallas, Texas, on November 22, 1963. A color 8 mm film that Muchmore photographed is one of the primary documents of the Kennedy assassination. The Muchmore film, with other 8 mm films taken by Abraham Zapruder and Orville Nix, was used by the Warren Commission to investigate the assassination and to position the presidential limousine in a forensic recreation of the event in May 1964.

Muchmore was born Marie Mobley in Ardmore, Oklahoma. Her mother was half Chickasaw Indian. One of her sisters, Aurelia, became a noted operatic soprano under the name Lushanya Mobley (1906–1990). Marie had no children.

Muchmore was an employee of "Justin McCarty Dress Manufacturer" in Dallas (707 Young Street which was four blocks south of the Texas School Book Depository), and was in Dealey Plaza with five other employees, including Wilma Bond, who had a still camera. She set up her 8 mm Keystone movie camera near the northwest corner of Main Street and Houston Street and awaited the president's arrival. The Muchmore film consists of seven sequences: six before the assassination, and one during the shooting. Muchmore began filming the presidential motorcade with her movie camera from her initial location near the northwest corner of Main Street and Houston Street as the motorcade turned onto Houston Street into Dealey Plaza. She then turned and walked with Wilma Bond several yards northwestward to again film the President's limousine as it went down Elm Street. Her film then captured the fatal head shot, seen from about 138 feet (42 m) away. The film ends seconds later as Secret Service agent Clint Hill, attempting to protect President Kennedy, runs to, then, quickly climbs board the accelerating limousine.

Muchmore sold the undeveloped film to the Dallas office of United Press International on November 25, 1963, for $1,000. It was processed by Kodak in Dallas, and flown to New York City. It appeared the following day on local television station WNEW-TV. The film now belongs to the Associated Press Television News, which restored it in 2002.

While visiting her family in Oklahoma for Thanksgiving, Muchmore told them about the film she had taken of the assassination; her family then told the FBI about the film. The FBI initially interviewed Muchmore in December 1963, during which she admitted she had a camera with her but denied that she took any pictures of the assassination scene. The FBI was unaware of the film's existence until a frame enlargement was published in the UPI book *Four Days: The Historical Record of the Death of President Kennedy* in January 1964. A subsequent FBI interview in February 1964 says:

Mrs. Muchmore stated that after the car turned on Elm Street from Houston Street, she heard a loud noise which at first she thought was a firecracker but then with the crowd of people running in all directions and hearing the two further noises, sounding like gunfire, she advised that she began to run to find a place to hide.

Source (edited): "http://en.wikipedia.org/wiki/Marie_Muchmore"

Marilyn Sitzman

Marilyn Sitzman (December 14, 1939, Lafayette, Colorado – August 11, 1993, Mesquite, Texas) was a witness to the assassination of U.S. President John F. Kennedy in Dallas, Texas on November 22, 1963. She was with her boss, Abraham Zapruder, as he made the Zapruder film, the most studied record of the assassination.

Zapruder's clothing company, Jennifer Juniors, was one block from Dealey Plaza, through which the presidential motorcade would be passing on November 22. When Zapruder arrived at work that morning without his 8 mm movie camera, his secretary Lillian Rogers encouraged him to go home to retrieve it. Zapruder, with Sitzman his receptionist standing behind him to steady him, filmed the presidential motorcade as both were standing on a 4-foot (1.2 m) high pedestal which extends from a retaining wall that was part of the John Neely Bryan concrete pergola on the grassy knoll north of Elm Street, in Dealey Plaza. The fatal head shot struck President Kennedy as his limousine passed almost directly in front of their position, 65 feet (20 m) from the center of Elm Street.

Sitzman; Emmett Hudson, who was standing on a stairway going up the grassy knoll; and Charles Hester, who was sitting on a bench in the pergola; were the only witnesses on the knoll who are on record about the direction of the shots they heard. All three said the shots came from the direction of the Texas School Book Depository. Sitzman rejected the theory that one or more shots came from behind the 5-foot (1.5 m) high stockade fence atop the knoll:

" And I'm sure that if the second shot would have come from a different place — and the supposed theory is they would have been much closer to me and on the right side — I would have heard the sounding of the gun much closer, and I probably had a ringing in my head because the fence was quite close to where we were standing, very close. "

Between Sitzman and the stockade fence was a 3.3-foot (1 m) high, L-shaped concrete alcove along the path from the stairway up the knoll to the area behind the pergola. Some assassination researchers, studying vague shapes in a photograph taken by Mary Moorman from across the street just after the fatal head shot, saw the so-called "badge man" aiming a rifle from this area. Another person, Gordon Arnold, came forth in 1978 to claim that he had been standing in that area taking a film of the motorcade.

However, in a long-forgotten interview with researcher Josiah Thompson from 1966, rediscovered in 1985, Sitzman gave eyewitness testimony to who was in the alcove below her and about nine yards (8.2 m) to her right: a young black couple was sitting on a bench, eating lunch and drinking sodas. When the shots rang out, the couple ran along the path to the area behind the pergola. Sitzman recalled hearing a soda bottle breaking as they ran. Asked if she saw anyone else in this area between the concrete wall and the stockade fence, Sitzman said no, only the couple.

Sitzman attended the University of Colorado at Boulder before moving to Dallas. She died of cancer at age 53.

Source (edited): "http://en.wikipedia.org/wiki/Marilyn_Sitzman"

Mary Moorman

Jean Hill (left) and Mary Moorman (right) as captured in Frame 298 of the Zapruder film, just less than one second before the fatal head shot

Mary Ann Moorman (born August 5, 1932) was a witness to the assassination of U.S. President John F. Kennedy. She is best known for her photograph capturing the presidential limousine a fraction of a second after the fatal shot.

Biography

Mary Moorman was born Mary Ann Boshart. She married Donald G. Moorman in 1952 and divorced him in 1973. She later married Gary Krahmer in 1980.

Assassination witness

Polaroid photo by Mary Moorman taken a fraction of a second after the fatal shot (detail)

On November 22, 1963, U.S. President John F. Kennedy was assassinated in Dallas, Texas.

Moorman was standing on grass about 2 feet (61 cm) south of the south curb of Elm Street in Dealey Plaza, directly across from the grassy knoll and the North Pergola concrete structure that Abraham Zapruder and his assistant Marilyn Sitzman were standing on, during the assassination. Moorman stated that she stepped off from the grass onto the street to take her Polaroid photo. Zapruder is seen standing on the pergola in the Moorman photograph, with the presidential limousine already having passed through the line of sight between Zapruder and Moorman.

Moorman was standing only 20 feet (6 m) behind and to the left of President Kennedy with her friend, Jean Hill, and they are clearly seen in many frames of the Zapruder film.

Between Zapruder film frames Z-315 and 316, approximately one sixth of a second after President Kennedy's head was shattered at frame Z-313, Moorman took a Polaroid photograph (her fifth that day) of the presidential limousine and President Kennedy that also includes the grassy knoll area.

Controversy

Polaroid Highlander Model 80A

What was captured in the background of the photo has been a matter of contentious debate. On the grassy knoll, some claim to have identified as many as four different figures, while others dismiss these indistinct images as trees or shadows. Most often a figure is identified as the "badge man" because the figure is supposedly a uniformed police officer. Others claim to see Gordon Arnold, a man who claimed to have filmed the assassination from that area, a man in a construction hard hat, and a hatted man behind the picket fence.

Moorman stated she heard a shot as the limousine passed her, then heard another shot or two after the president's head first exploded. She stated that she could not determine where the shots came from, and that she saw no one in the area that appeared to have possibly been the assassin. Moorman was interviewed by the Dallas County Sheriff's Department and the FBI. She was called by the Warren Commission to testify, but due to a sprained ankle, she was unable to be questioned. She was never contacted by them again.

Source (edited): "http://en.wikipedia.org/wiki/Mary_Moorman"

Nellie Connally

Idanell Brill "Nellie" Connally (February 24, 1919 – September 1, 2006) was the First Lady of Texas from 1963 to 1969.

First Lady of Texas

Born in Austin, Texas, she was wife of John Connally, who served as Governor of Texas and later as Secretary of the Treasury.

Death of President Kennedy

JFK, Jackie, and the Connallys in the presidential limousine before the assassination

At the time of her death in 2006, she was the last surviving occupant of the presidential limousine that carried John F. Kennedy when he was assassinated in Dallas, Texas, on November 22, 1963. In addition to the President, she was predeceased by her husband and by First Lady Jacqueline Kennedy, as well as by Roy Kellerman and William Greer, the two secret service agents operating the limousine and seated in front of the Connallys. Secret Service agent Clint Hill was not an original passenger in the limousine; however, he boarded the vehicle after shots were fired and remained until the car's arrival at Parkland Hospital, making him the last surviving passenger that rode in the limousine that day.

While riding in the car with President Kennedy, she told him, "Mr. President, you can't say Dallas doesn't love you." Almost immediately, she heard the first of what she later concluded were three gunshots in quick succession.

The President and Mrs. Connally's husband were shot, resulting in fatal wounds to the President and serious wounds to Governor Connally. Mrs. Connally got down in the car to take care of her husband, who had slumped after the second shot. "I never looked back again. I was just trying to take care of him", she said.

Connally had said the most enduring image she had of the assassination in Dallas was of a mixture of blood and roses.

"It's the image of yellow roses and red roses and blood all over the car ... all over us", she said in a 2003 interview with The Associated Press. "I'll never forget it. ... It was so quick and so short, so potent."

Anniversaries and media interviews followed the Connallys for decades to come. In her 2003 book *From Love Field—Our Final Hours with John F. Kennedy*, Connally shared her personal diary of the event, originally written for her children and other descendants in the days immediately after the assassination.

Diabetes Advocate

She was also an active fundraiser for many charities. In 1989, Richard Nixon, Donald Trump, and Barbara Walters turned out for a gala to honor her and raise money for diabetes research.

"I've never known a woman with Super Nellie's courage, compassion and character," Walters said. "For all her ups and downs, I've never heard a self-pitying word from her." The "downs" that Walters spoke of were financial difficulties she and her husband faced.

Bankruptcy

Private business ventures after 1980 were less successful than John Connally's career as a politician and dealmaking Houston lawyer. An oil company in which he invested encountered trouble, and $200 million of real-estate projects failed. He filed for reorganization of his personal finances under Chapter 11 of the federal bankruptcy code and for liquidation, under Chapter 7, of the Barnes–Connally Partnership, the Austin-based real-estate venture that he founded with former Lt. Gov. Ben Barnes. The auction paid only a fraction of the $93 million in debts that Connally listed with the bankruptcy court in Austin.

Breast Cancer Advocate

Nellie Connally celebrated her 80th birthday with fellow breast cancer survivors at a ceremony in the Nellie B. Connally Breast Center at Anderson Hospital in Houston. She had been free of breast cancer for 10 years. She served on the M. D. Anderson Board of Visitors since 1984, and a fund in her name raised millions for research and patient programs.

Death

She died in her sleep at Westminster Manor in Austin, aged 87.

Children

The Connallys had four children, Kathleen (who predeceased both her parents), John B. Connally III, Sharon Connally, and Mark Madison Connally. Source (edited): "http://en.wikipedia.org/wiki/Nellie_Connally"

Orville Nix

Orville Orhel Nix (April 16, 1911 – January 17, 1972, Dallas, Texas) was a witness to the assassination of U.S. President John F. Kennedy in Dallas, Texas, on November 22, 1963. His filming of the event is considered nearly as important as the more famous Abraham Zapruder film.

Nix worked for the General Services Administration as an air conditioning engineer in the former Terminal Annex building on the south side of Dealey Plaza. He filmed with an 8 mm movie camera, first from the southwest corner of Main and Houston streets, then from the south side of Main Street 50 feet (15 m) west of Houston, then from a point about another 50 feet west. The footage contains three scenes: the motorcade entering Dealey Plaza, the last shot of the assassination in front of the grassy knoll along Elm Street, and the panic and confusion afterward.

The Nix film was obtained as a result of a notice that the FBI gave to film processing plants in the Dallas area, that the FBI would be interested in obtaining or knowing about any film they processed relating to the assassination. When Nix heard about this from his processor, he delivered the film to the FBI office in Dallas on December 1, 1963. It was returned to him three days later.

United Press International purchased the copyright for $5,000 and took possession of the original film from Nix on December 6, 1963. UPI distributed frame enlargements to its news subscribers the following day. The original was examined by the House Select Committee on Assassinations in 1978. When UPI returned the copyright and all its copies to the Nix family in 1992, the original film was missing. In 2002, the Nix family assigned the copyright of the film to the Dallas County Historical Foundation, which operates the Sixth Floor Museum at Dealey Plaza.

Nix was interviewed in 1966 by investigator Mark Lane for his documentary *Rush to Judgment*. In a filmed interview undertaken by Lane, he also stated that the film he received back was not identical to the one that he shot. He told Lane that at the time of the assassination, he believed that the shots came from behind the fence on the grassy knoll, but was later told that conclusive proof existed that shots only came from the Texas School Book Depository and that he was convinced by this. He was also interviewed by CBS News in 1967 for a television documentary on the Kennedy assassination.
Source (edited): "http://en.wikipedia.org/wiki/Orville_Nix"

Phillip Willis

Phillip LaFrance Willis (2 August 1918, Kaufman County, Texas – 27 January 1995, Dallas, Texas) was a close witness to the assassination of President Kennedy.

Willis served in the United States Army Air Forces during World War II, and as a young lieutenant he was present at the Japanese attack on Pearl Harbor in 1941. Because of a back injury he suffered when he was shot down over the Pacific, Willis retired in 1946 as a highly decorated Major. He earned a bachelor's degree in government at North Texas State Teachers College in 1948. He was elected to the Texas House of Representatives in 1946 and 1948. He later became a Lincoln automobile dealer, and an independent real estate broker. He moved to Dallas in 1960.

Clearly seen in the Zapruder film at the start of the assassination, Willis was wearing a dark colored suit and tie, standing at the Elm Street south curb to the presidential limousine's left, directly across from the Texas School Book Depository.

During the assassination, Willis snapped a 35mm color slide (the fifth of twenty-seven he captured in Dealey Plaza that day) showing the presidential limousine and its occupants, the United States Secret Service agents' follow-up car and occupants, parade onlookers, and the grassy knoll visible in the background.

Willis testified to the Warren Commission that his fifth photo was inadvertently snapped when, just after he had prepared his 35mm Argus camera to capture a photo, he was suddenly startled by a gunshot related noise (the first of three shots he remembered hearing), and his finger that was already on the camera shutter button reacted to the gunshot related noise, then, he quickly depressed the button and the fifth photo was captured. As documented by the House Select Committee on Assassinations, this fifth photo was captured concurrent with Zapruder film frame 202. (The Warren Commission and subsequent investigations have all determined that President Kennedy was hidden by a very large oak tree from the view of anyone firing a weapon from the sniper's lair on the 6th floor of the Texas School Book Depository from Z-160 through Z-206.)

In his fifth photo, some conspiracists allege that the image of a still-unknown person can be seen located up on the grassy knoll, seen near a 3-foot-tall concrete wall and near the 5-foot-tall stockade fence. The angled shape of this still-unknown person's outline has led to that person's image being labeled by authors in books and persons working in the Kennedy assassination research community the "black dog man."

In 1978, when Willis's daughter Rosemary was interviewed by investigators from the House Select Committee on Assassinations, she stated to the HSCA that her father became upset when the Dallas policemen, sheriffs, and detectives—who first quickly ran onto the grassy knoll where Phillip thought the shots came from—then ran away from the grassy knoll. In Willis's Warren Commission testimony he stated that shots came from the Texas School Book Depository.

In 1988 Willis stated on camera in the UK 1988 Independent Television Company [ITV] documentary, "The Men Who Killed Kennedy," that during his Warren Commission testimony all the Commission wanted to hear about was that Willis heard three shots that probably originated from the depository, but that for President Kennedy's fatal head shot Willis stated, "So I am very dead certain that, at least, one shot, including the one that took the president's skull off, had to come from the right front, and, I'll stand by that to my death."

When Willis died in 1995, the Texas House passed a resolution to honor him.
Source (edited): "http://en.wikipedia.org/wiki/Phillip_Willis"

Ralph Yarborough

Ralph Webster Yarborough (June 8, 1903 – January 27, 1996) was a Texas Democratic politician who served in the

United States Senate (1957 to 1971) and was a leader of the progressive or liberal wing of his party in his many races for statewide office. As a United States Senator, he was a staunch supporter and author of "Great Society" legislation that encompassed Medicare and Medicaid, the War on Poverty, federal support for higher education and veterans. He co-wrote the Endangered Species Act and was the only southern senator to vote for all civil rights bills from 1957 to 1970 (including the Civil Rights Act of 1964 and the Voting Rights Act of 1965). Yarborough was known as "Smilin' Ralph" and used the slogan *"Let's put the jam on the lower shelf so the little people can reach it"* in his campaigns.

Early life and career

Yarborough was born in Chandler in Henderson County west of Tyler, the seventh of Charles Richard Yarborough and the former Nannie Jane Spear's nine children. He was appointed to West Point in 1919 but dropped out to become a teacher. Yarborough attended Sam Houston State Teachers College and worked his way into the University of Texas at Austin. He graduated from the University of Texas Law School in 1927 and practiced law in El Paso until he was hired as an assistant attorney general in 1931 by the state Attorney General James V. Allred.

Yarborough was an expert in Texas land law and specialized in prosecuting major oil companies that violated production limits or failed to pay oil royalties to the Permanent School Fund for drilling on public lands. He earned renown for winning a million dollar judgment against the Mid-Kansas Oil and Gas Company for oil royalties, the second largest judgment ever in Texas at the time. After Allred was elected governor, he appointed Yarborough to the bench in 1936, making him the 53rd District judge for Austin's Travis County. Yarborough was confirmed in that office by an election later the same year. Yarborough's first run for state office resulted in a third-place finish in the Democratic primary for state attorney general in 1938 against the sitting lieutenant governor. He served in the U.S. Army during World War II after 1943 and achieved the rank of lieutenant colonel.

Running for governor

Yarborough was urged to run again for state attorney general in 1952, and he planned to do so until he received a personal affront from Governor Allan Shivers who told him not to run. Texas Secretary of State John Ben Shepperd resigned in the spring of 1952 and was elected attorney general that year. He served two two-year terms. Angered at Shivers, Yarborough ran in the gubernatorial primaries in 1952 and 1954 against the conservative Shivers, drawing support from labor unions and liberals. Yarborough denounced the corrupt "Shivercrats" for veterans' fraud in the General Land Office and for endorsing in 1952 and 1956 the Republican Eisenhower/Nixon ticket, instead of the Democrat Adlai Stevenson of Illinois. Shivers portrayed Yarborough as an integrationist supported by communists and labor unions. The 1954 election was particularly nasty in its race-baiting by Shivers as it was the year that *Brown v. Board of Education* was decided, and Shivers made the most of the court decision in order to play on voters' fears. Yarborough, however, nearly upset Shivers.

In 1956, Yarborough made it to the primary runoff for governor against U.S. Senator Price Daniel. Texas historian J. Evetts Haley ran in the primary to the political right of both Daniel and Yarborough but polled few votes. After being endorsed by former opponent and former Governor W. Lee O'Daniel, and making aggressive attacks on the Shivers-backed candidate, Yarborough looked to win the runoff, but instead he trailed Daniel by about nine thousand votes. It is believed (by Yarborough, his supporters, and biographer) that the election was stolen because of irregular voting in East Texas and that Yarborough really won the runoff by thirty thousand. Nevertheless, Yarborough's runs for governor had raised his stature and popularity in the state as he had been campaigning for six straight years for office.

Becoming a Senator

When Daniel resigned from the Senate in 1957 to become governor, Yarborough ran in the special election to fill the empty seat. With no runoff then required, he needed only a plurality of votes to win. Ironically, his many runs for governor made him the best positioned candidate. Yarborough won the special election with 38 percent of the vote to join fellow Texan Lyndon B. Johnson in the Senate.

In office, Ralph Yarborough was a very different kind of Southern senator. He refused to sign the Southern Manifesto opposing integration and supported national Democratic goals of more funding for health care, education, and the environment. Himself a veteran, he worked to expand the G.I. Bill to Cold War veterans.

In 1958, Ralph Yarborough easily defeated conservative William A. Blakley of Dallas, who was backed by Yarborough's long-time party rival, Governor Daniel, in the Democratic primary and then cruised to victory in the general election against Republican Roy Whittenburg of Amarillo. In 1962, Whittenburg ran unsuccessfully for governor in the Republican primary against Jack Cox of Houston, who would in turn lose to Yarborough's intraparty rival, John Connally. During his first full term, Yarborough worked for a bill signed by President John F. Kennedy to designate Padre Island as a national seashore.

Ralph Yarborough rode in the Dallas motorcade where John F. Kennedy was assassinated on November 22, 1963. Yarborough was in the same convertible as Vice President Lyndon B. Johnson, Lady Bird Johnson, and United States Secret Service agent Rufus Youngblood, who protected all three of them with his body when shots were fired at Kennedy. only two cars away from the presidential limousine. A sobbing Yarborough announced Kennedy's death at Parkland Memorial Hospital by saying: "Excalibur has sunk beneath the waves."

In 1964, Yarborough again won the

primary without a runoff and went on to general election victory with 56.2 percent in LBJ's 1964 Democratic landslide. His Republican Party (GOP) opponent was future president George H. W. Bush who attacked Yarborough as a left-wing demagogue and for his vote in favor of the Civil Rights Act of 1964. Yarborough denounced Bush as an extremist to the right of that year's GOP nominee for president Barry M. Goldwater and as a rich easterner and a carpetbagger trying to buy a Senate seat. It has since been learned that then Governor Connally was covertly aiding Bush instead of party nominee Yarborough against President Johnson's wishes by teaching the techniques of split ticket voting. In that same election, Connally easily defeated Bush's ticket-mate, Jack Crichton, a Dallas oil and natural gas industrialist.

Although Yarborough supported Johnson's domestic agenda, he went public with his criticism of Johnson's foreign policy and the Vietnam War after Johnson announced his retirement. Yarborough supported Robert F. Kennedy until his assassination, then supported Eugene McCarthy until his loss in Chicago, and finally backed Hubert Humphrey for President in the pivotal campaign of 1968. In 1969, Senator Yarborough became chairman of the Senate Committee on Labor and Public Welfare.

Defeat

In 1970, South Texan businessman and former Congressman Lloyd Bentsen, won a 54% to 46% upset victory against Yarborough in the Democratic primary, when Yarborough was focusing on the general election again against Bush. Bentsen played on voters' fears of societal breakdown and urban riots and made an issue of Yarborough's opposition to the Vietnam War. Bentsen said that Yarborough was a political antique. Said Bentsen, "It would be nice if Ralph Yarborough would vote for his state every once in a while." Bentsen went on to win the general election against George H.W. Bush.

In 1972, Ralph Yarborough made a comeback effort to win the Democratic nomination for U.S. Senator as a challenger of Republican Senator John Tower, who as a young man had once circulated Ralph Yarborough stickers. Yarborough won the first round of the primary and came within 526 votes of winning the primary runoff. Yarborough again made accusations of vote fraud from the conservative wing. He lost in the primary runoff to a former U.S. Attorney, Barefoot Sanders, in an anti-incumbent sweep after the Sharpstown Bank-stock Scandal despite neither being an incumbent nor involved at all with the scandal.

Ralph Yarborough never again sought public office.

Yarborough monument at Texas State Cemetery in Austin, Texas

Death

Yarborough died in 1996 in Austin. He is interred at the Texas State Cemetery there beside his wife, the former Opal Warren (1903-2002), a native of Murchison in Henderson County, Texas. The Texas State Cemeterty is sometimes called "the Arlington of Texas." Also buried there are Yarborough's old intraparty rivals, Allan Shivers and John Connally. Yarborough left a legacy in the modernization of the state of Texas and achieved political power when Texas had a native son, Lyndon Johnson, in the White House. He was combative with the dominant industries of oil and natural gas and pushed for the petroleum industry to pay a greater share of taxes.

Legacy

Yarborough also was one of the last of the New Deal Democrats and powerful liberals in Texas state politics. (He was followed by the moderately liberal Bentsen and the conservative Phil Gramm). Yarborough is remembered as the acknowledged "patron saint of Texas liberals." Supporters and former aides that have since risen to prominence include Jim Hightower, Ann Richards, and Garry Mauro.

The University of Texas at Austin Press published a biography titled, *Ralph W. Yarborough: The People's Senator*, by Patrick L. Cox. It features a foreword written by Sen. Edward Kennedy (D-MA).

The Yarborough Branch of the Austin Public Library was named in Ralph Yarborough's honor.

Source (edited): "http://en.wikipedia.org/wiki/Ralph_Yarborough"

Robert MacNeil

Robert Breckenridge Ware MacNeil, OC, known sometimes as **Robin MacNeil**, (born January 19, 1931), is currently a novelist and formerly was a television news anchor and journalist who had paired with Jim Lehrer to create *The MacNeil/Lehrer Report* in 1975.

Early life

MacNeil was born in Montreal, the son of Margaret Virginia (née Oxner) and Robert A. S. MacNeil. He was raised in Halifax, Nova Scotia, went to boarding school at Upper Canada College, then attended Dalhousie University and later graduated from Carleton University in Ottawa in 1955. He began working in the news field at ITV in London, then for Reuters and then for NBC News as a correspondent in Washington, D.C. and New York City.

Career

On November 22, 1963, MacNeil was

covering President Kennedy's visit to Dallas for NBC News. After shots rang out in Dealey Plaza MacNeil, who was with the presidential motorcade, followed crowds running onto the Grassy Knoll (he appears in a photo taken just moments after the assassination). He then headed towards the nearest building and encountered a man leaving the Texas School Book Depository. He asked the man where the nearest telephone was and the man pointed and went on his way. MacNeil later learned the man he encountered at about 12:33 p.m. CST may have been Lee Harvey Oswald. This conclusion was made by historian William Manchester in his book *The Death of a President* (1967), who believed that Oswald, recounting the day's events to the Dallas police, mistook MacNeil as a Secret Service agent because of his suit, blond crew cut, and press badge (which Oswald apparently mistook for government identification). For his part, MacNeil says "it was possible, but I had no way of confirming that either of the young men I had spoken to was Oswald." On the phone, MacNeil relayed the first report of the shooting to Jim Holton of NBC Radio, who recorded MacNeil's records of what had happened. MacNeil then headed to Parkland Hospital where he arranged a phone connection with Frank McGee, who was anchoring the developments with Bill Ryan and Chet Huntley from NBC-TV in New York. At approximately 1:40 PM CST, MacNeil relayed to McGee that White House acting press secretary Malcolm Kilduff made the official announcement that President Kennedy had died at 1:00 CST. That evening, MacNeil went to Dallas police headquarters and saw Oswald twice at close range, including when Oswald said "I'm just a patsy," but he did not recognize Oswald.

Beginning in 1967, MacNeil covered American and European politics for the BBC and has served as the host for the news discussion show *Washington Week in Review*. MacNeil rose to fame during his coverage of the Senate Watergate hearings for PBS, which led to an Emmy Award. This helped lead to his most famous news role, where he worked with Jim Lehrer to create *The Robert MacNeil Report* in 1975. This was later renamed *The MacNeil/Lehrer Report* and then *The MacNeil/Lehrer NewsHour*. MacNeil retired on October 20, 1995.

On September 11, 2001, after the terrorist attacks in New York and Washington, he called PBS, asking if he could help them with their coverage of the attacks. He helped PBS in its coverage of the attacks and the aftermath, interviewing reporters, and giving his thoughts on the attacks.

He hosted the PBS television show *America at a Crossroads*, which ran from April 15-20, 2007.

In the late 1990s, he discussed openly his son's homosexuality, saying it could help other fathers to know how he dealt with the fact in a positive way.

In a *Sesame Street* Special Report, *The Muppet Show* parody of the Iran-Contra scandal, MacNeil investigated the "Cookiegate" incident involving the Cookie Monster.

Robert MacNeil became a U.S. citizen in 1997 and "[i]n January 1998, he was made an officer in the Order of Canada."

Source (edited): "http://en.wikipedia.org/wiki/Robert_MacNeil"

Rosemary Willis

Rosemary Willis (born 1953) was a close witness during the assassination of President Kennedy.

Clearly seen in the Zapruder film at the start of the assassination wearing a white, hooded coat and a red skirt, located to the limousine's left, she runs southwestward and parallel with the limousine while she faces for a short time when the limousine was to her direct right.

At circa Zapruder film frame 190 (hereafter "Z-190"), she is seen slowing, then she stops running and, simultaneous with her slowing/stopping, she slightly turns her level-facing head to end up looking towards the southwest corner of the Texas School Book Depository.

Immediately after the sitting upright President Kennedy is first hidden at Z-207 by the "Stemmons Freeway" traffic sign in the Zapruder film, Rosemary suddenly, and beginning at Z-214, snaps her head very rapidly 90 to 100 degrees westward --completely away from the depository southwest corner-- within only 0.16 second to then face Abraham Zapruder and the grassy knoll by Z-217.

Precisely 0.60 second after starting her extremely quick westward headsnap towards Mr. Zapruder and the grassy knoll, President Kennedy's head then emerges back into the Zapruder film view at Z-225 still sitting upright with his face and arms already displaying a physical reaction to having already been impacted by a bullet.

Importantly, in 1978 Rosemary was interviewed by investigators from the House Select Committee on Assassinations and stated that she heard at least 4 shots during the assassination. She also stated to the HSCA that while she was still facing the grassy knoll picket fence, she was attracted to view the quick movement of a person who quickly dropped down behind a "wall" out of her view. Rosemary was also documented in the HSCA report that her father, military veteran Phillip Willis, became upset when the Dallas policemen, sheriffs, and detectives --who first quickly ran onto the grassy knoll where he thought the shots came from-- then the authorities ran away from the grassy knoll.

Rosemary's sister, Linda, stated to assassination researcher and author Richard Trask ("Pictures of the Pain" 1994) that after the assassination she and Rosemary also saw someone find a piece of the president's head that had landed in the grass located at least twenty-two feet to the left of the president.

After the assassination Willis, along with her sister, father (Phillip), and mother (Marilyn) were present at the Kodak photographic laboratory getting her father's assassination related photo slides developed when the Zapruder film was also developed and first shown to approximately nineteen persons.

Rosemary Willis was never called to testify to the Warren Commission. Source (edited): "http://en.wikipedia.org/wiki/Rosemary_Willis"

Roy Kellerman

Roy Herman Kellerman (March 14, 1915 – March 22, 1984) was a U.S. Secret Service Agent assigned to protect President John F. Kennedy when he was assassinated on November 22, 1963. In his reports, later testimony and interviews, Kellerman outlines in detail his role in the immediate aftermath of the assassination, controlling key evidence of the crime and guiding doctors during the official autopsy at Bethesda Naval Hospital.

History

Kellerman, a Macomb County, Michigan native, graduated from high school in 1933 and worked for the Dodge division of Chrysler sporadically from 1935 until 1937 when he was sworn in as a trooper for the Michigan State Police. Kellerman joined the Secret Service in Detroit just before Christmas, 1941, transferring temporarily to the White House detail in March 1942 and permanently one month later. After the assassination, he was promoted, retiring from the Secret Service in 1968 as an assistant administrator. He died in St. Petersburg, Florida on March 22, 1984 of unreported causes.

Actions during assassination

As the Assistant Special Agent in Charge of November 22, 1963 Shift Team #3, Kellerman was riding in the front passenger seat of the presidential limousine. The driver was Secret Service Agent William Greer. Like all Secret Service agents assigned to protect the President of the United States, Kellerman was trained to use his own body as a shield, taking a bullet if necessary in the line of duty.

Kellerman was the nearest agent to the President during the attack. In the uncropped Zapruder film, he can be seen turning his entire torso to view Kennedy at a time when the president shows distress. Then, he turns back around to face forward in a relaxed position, which he maintains as the remaining shots are fired into the president and the limo speeds away from the scene.

The recently stabilized version of the Zapruder film displays even greater detail of Kellerman's actions during the shooting, including his raising a radio handset and an apparent momentary glance at Greer. Both actions take place after Kennedy is seen to be in distress but before the fatal head shot.

Kellerman testified to the Warren Commission, "I turned around to find out what happened when two additional shots rang out and the President slumped into Mrs. Kennedy's lap and Governor Connally fell to Mrs. Connally's lap." As clearly seen in the Zapruder film and Ike Altgens photo number six, Kellerman did not start his head turn rearward until Zapruder film frame 253 to 254.

Kellerman also testified to the Warren Commission, "I am going to say that I have, from the firecracker report and the two other shots that I know, those were three shots. But, if President Kennedy had from all reports four wounds, Governor Connally three, there have got to be more than three shots, gentlemen."

He further testified to the Warren Commission that after he remembered hearing the first audible muzzle blast or mechanically suppressed fired bullet bow shockwave, the assassination then ended in a "flurry of shells" coming into the limousine that reminded him of a jet sonic-boom sound quickness.

Controller of evidence

Kellerman's report and later testimony indicate that he was with the president without interruption from the motorcade's departure from Love Field, through the entire autopsy and embalming and up until the president's remains were brought back to the White House. In photographs and footage of the casket being loaded aboard Air Force One at Love Field, and later upon its arrival at Andrews Air Force Base, Kellerman can be seen directing the movements of the president's casket.

Kellerman maintained his composure immediately after the violent death of the president he was charged to protect, managing events as they continued to develop. Kellerman testified that he played a role in the autopsy at Bethesda, including guiding the doctors toward specific conclusions regarding bullet locations. Kellerman also took personal custody of the x-rays and photographic negatives at the conclusion of the autopsy and took them with him as he rode in the ambulance that transported the president's casket to the White House. When asked by the House Select Committee on Assassinations staff why he wanted this material, he said "...the point is, he was our man, everything belonged in the White House."."

With Kellerman in charge of local events (and with the assistance of Greer), the Secret Service maintained custody of the most important evidence of the crime, including the president's body, clothing, limousine, forensic tissues, and autopsy photographs and X-rays, returning everything to the White House before the sun rose on November 23, 1963, less than fifteen hours from when the first shot was fired.

According to his widow June, Roy Kellerman believed there was a conspiracy behind the death of JFK.."

In Pop Culture

A reference to Roy Kellerman can be found in the hit TV series "Prison Break". In the show Special Agent Paul Kellerman is a secret service agent who is deeply involved in covering up a government conspiracy.

Source (edited): "http://en.wikipedia.org/wiki/Roy_Kellerman"

Umbrella Man (JFK assassination)

Assassination of JFK aftermath at Dealey Plaza; The Umbrella Man is sitting next to the road sign (the man on the right site)

The **Umbrella Man** is a man who appears in the Zapruder film, and several other films and photographs at the Stemmons Freeway sign during the JFK assassination within Dealey Plaza.

Conspiracy

An unknown person popularly dubbed "The Umbrella Man" has been the object of much speculation, as he was the only person seen carrying and opening an umbrella on that 66-degree, sunny day. As President John F. Kennedy's limousine approached the umbrella man, the man opened up and lifted the umbrella high above his head, then spun or panned the umbrella from east to west (clockwise) as the president approached and passed by him.

Some have claimed that the Umbrella Man was involved in the Kennedy assassination. One commonly held theory is that the Umbrella Man was signaling the shooters, and he is depicted this way in both Oliver Stone's film *JFK* and an episode of the "The X-Files." A less common theory, held by L. Fletcher Prouty and others, is that the umbrella contained a poison dart fired at Kennedy to immobilize President Kennedy's muscles (his movements are seen to freeze and cease within two seconds of Z-225).

Witt

After an appeal to the public by the United States House Select Committee on Assassinations, **Louie Steven Witt** came forward in 1978 and claimed to be the Umbrella Man. He claimed he still had that umbrella and did not know he had been the subject of controversy. He said that he brought the umbrella to simply heckle Kennedy. John Kennedy's father had been a supporter of the Nazi-appeasing British Prime Minister Neville Chamberlain. By waving a black umbrella, Chamberlain's trademark fashion accessory, Witt claims he was protesting the Kennedy family appeasing Adolf Hitler before World War II. An umbrella had been used in cartoons in the 1930s to symbolize such appeasement. Kennedy, who wrote a thesis on appeasement while at Harvard, Why England Slept, might have recognized the symbolism of the umbrella.

Testifying before the HSCA, Witt said "I think if the *Guinness Book of World Records* had a category for people who were at the wrong place at the wrong time, doing the wrong thing, I would be No. 1 in that position, without even a close runner-up." Some conspiracy theorists are still skeptical of Witt's story, however, and do not believe him to be the true "Umbrella Man."

Some claim that a dark skinned man standing very close to the Umbrella Man between the Umbrella Man and President Kennedy was an assassination accomplice. At Zapruder film frame Z-202 this dark-skinned man was photographed facing the on-coming president with both arms down. By Z-225 (slightly over one second later) the same dark-skinned man shot his right hand upward quickly and extended in an apparent wave (even though his hand remains un-waving, suggesting a "Nazi salute"). In photos afterward, some theorize that the same dark-skinned man was photographed speaking into a walkie-talkie, and other photos seem to show something bulging noticeably from his back pants pocket. Witt claims he never noticed that the dark-skinned man near him was holding anything.

Source (edited): "http://en.wikipedia.org/wiki/Umbrella_Man_(JFK_assassination)"

William Allen Harper

William Allen Harper was a Texas Christian University medical student who, after the assassination of President John F. Kennedy, discovered a large piece of President Kennedy's skull bone in the grass to the left of President Kennedy and 117' forward of his location when he was first shot in the head.

After discovering the "Harper fragment" at 5:30 PM CDT on November 25, 1963, Harper gave the skull piece to his uncle, Jack C. Harper, a medical doctor at the Methodist Hospital in Dallas, who in turn gave the skull piece to A. B. Cairns, the Chief Pathologist at the same hospital. On November 25, Cairns gave the skull piece to FBI Special Agent James W. Anderton and it was then sent to the FBI Laboratory in Washington DC. The Harper fragment is not currently locatable within the physical evidence from the assassination.

Source (edited): "http://en.wikipedia.org/wiki/William_Allen_Harper"

William Greer

William Robert Greer (September 22, 1909 – February 23, 1985) was an agent of the U.S. Secret Service, best known for having driven President John F. Kennedy's automobile in the motorcade through Dealey Plaza in Dallas on November 22, 1963, when the president was assassinated.

History

Greer was born on a farm in Stewartstown, County Tyrone, Ireland, and emigrated to the United States in 1929. After working for over a decade as a chauffeur and servant to several wealthy families in the Boston area, including the Lodge family, Greer enlisted in the U.S. Navy in World War II, and then joined the United States Secret Service on October 1, 1945.

Greer took a role close to Kennedy, and can be seen in several pictures with the Kennedy family. He chauffeured the president on many occasions, including the day of the assassination. Like all agents involved, he has been the target of much speculation and criticism for his actions on that day. He testified before the Warren Commission regarding the incident.

Greer retired on disability from the Secret Service in 1966 due to a stomach ulcer that grew worse following the Kennedy assassination. In 1973 he relocated to Waynesville, North Carolina, where he eventually died of cancer. Greer's son Richard told author Vince Palamara in 1991 that his father "had absolutely no survivor's guilt."

Analysis and criticism

Some commentators have criticized Greer's actions during the assassination, noting that he did not accelerate the vehicle to get the president out of danger as soon as he could have. In the confusion after the first shot was fired, the limousine's brake lights can be seen coming on briefly, slowing the car to almost a walking pace. The vehicle accelerated several seconds later, but by then the fatal shot had been fired. (Since that time, Secret Service agents have been trained to accelerate rapidly out of the area if they even think they hear gunfire.)

Greer did not discuss slowing the car in his statement to the FBI on the night of the assassination, nor did he mention this aspect to the Warren Commission during the official investigation. His testimony seems to deny that he turned to look directly at Kennedy during the shooting, although the Zapruder film shows him doing so. Secret Service procedures in place at the time did not allow Greer to take action without orders from senior agent Roy Kellerman, who sat to Greer's right. Kellerman has stated that he shouted, "Let's get out of line, we've been hit," but that Greer apparently turned to look at Kennedy, initiating a fatal delay, before accelerating the car out of the danger zone. As Roy Kellerman told author William Manchester, "Greer then looked in the back of the car. Maybe he didn't believe me."

No agents were reprimanded or disciplined for their actions during the shooting, but privately, Jacqueline Kennedy was bitterly critical of the agents' performance, Greer's in particular, comparing his efforts to those of "Maud Shaw" (the Kennedy children's nanny). Greer later delivered a heartfelt apology to her.

Source (edited): "http://en.wikipedia.org/wiki/William_Greer"